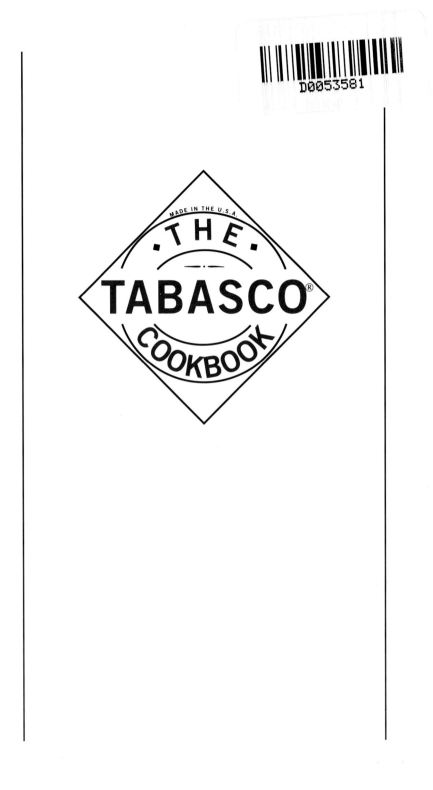

MADE IN THE U.S.A.

·THE·

TABASCO®

COOKBOOK

More than 300 Tabasco sauce bottles whirl through filling machines each minute.

We love y

Happy Happy
Father's Day to a
man who likes
to "spice" it up!

♡ xo
"

125 Years of America's Favorite Pepper Sauce

BY PAUL McILHENNY WITH
BARBARA HUNTER

GRAMERCY BOOKS
NEW YORK

Copyright © 1993 by Paul McIlhenny with Barbara Hunter

This 2004 edition is published by Gramercy Books, an imprint of
Random House Value Publishing, a division of Random House,
Inc., New York, by arrangement with Crown Publishers, a division
of Random House, Inc.

Gramercy is a registered trademark and the colophon is a
trademark of Random House, Inc.

TABASCO® is a registered trademark of McIlhenny Company,
Avery Island, LA 70513.

Random House
New York • Toronto • London • Sydney • Auckland
www.randomhouse.com

Design by Renato Stanisic

Printed and bound in the Singapore

A catalog record for this title is available from
the Library of Congress.

ISBN 0-517-22334-1

10 9 8 7 6 5 4 3 2 1

Above: The three-year
aging process in
white oak barrels gives
Tabasco sauce its unique
flavor. Opposite: The
"laboratory" on Avery
Island where Edmund
McIlhenny first
produced Tabasco sauce
after the Civil War.

We dedicate this book to members
of the McIlhenny family who have preserved and nurtured
our famous pepper sauce, and to generations of
employees, distributors, and others who have taken such pride
in producing Tabasco sauce and making it
available throughout this world—and even in outer space.

CONTENTS

Introduction 9

Soups & Starters 13

Breakfast & Brunch 35

Entrées 53

Vegetables & Side Dishes 101

Condiments & Sauces 127

Mail Order Suppliers . 142

Index . . . 143

INTRODUCTION

Time was when you could tell the length of a marriage by the level of Tabasco pepper sauce left in the bottle. Not anymore. The distinctive piquant flavor of everyone's favorite pepper sauce has firmly established it as a staple ingredient in contemporary cooking. But most people don't realize that there are 125 years of history in every little red bottle, going all the way back to the Civil War.

It all began on Avery Island, one of five islands rising in mystical fashion above the flat Louisiana Gulf coast. The island literally sits atop a mountain of solid salt, once supplying quantities of this valuable commodity to the Confederate states, but when Union forces invaded the island in 1863 the saltworks were totally destroyed.

After the war, my great-grandfather, Edmund McIlhenny, known to us as Grandpère, returned to the island. An avid gardener, he had been carefully nurturing a special variety of red capsicum peppers from Mexico. Grandpère delighted in the spicy flavor of these special peppers, which had, surprisingly, survived the general devastation of the island.

Above: An 1857 portrait of Edmund McIlhenny, better known as Grandpère, who first created Tabasco sauce in 1868.

He experimented with making a pepper sauce by crushing the ripest, reddest peppers, adding half a coffee cup of Avery Island salt per gallon, and letting the concoction age in crockery jars. When thirty days had passed, he added "the best French wine vinegar" and, occasionally stirring each batch carefully by hand, let the mixture age for another thirty days so the flavors could intermingle.

After straining the sauce, he filled small cologne-type bottles with a sprinkler fitting; the bottles were then corked and dipped in green sealing wax.

"That Famous Sauce Mr. McIlhenny Makes" lent welcome excitement to the monotonous diet of the Reconstruction South, and before long it was in such demand that he decided to market it commercially. In 1868 Grand-père sent 350 bottles of his pepper sauce under the trademark Tabasco to a carefully selected group of U.S. wholesalers, and, to his delight, the orders poured in.

Today, when the demand for spicy, well-seasoned food is even greater, people appreciate the fact that the aged capsicum peppers used for Tabasco sauce give it a richer flavor, as well as a higher heat level, than most other sauces. In fact, Tabasco sauce scores 9,000 to 12,000 units on the Scoville scale, the standardized yardstick of hotness in food, while many of the others make it only to 3,000 units. And while less potent sauces often compensate for their lack of flavor and heat with more salt, Tabasco sauce has about 2 mg. sodium per $\frac{1}{16}$ teaspoon, a fifth to a quarter that of other pepper sauces, making it a great way to enhance flavors while reducing added sodium.

Tabasco sauce is still made today much as it was in Grandpère's time. Ripe peppers are crushed immediately after harvest, mixed with Avery Island salt, and aged in white oak barrels for up to three years. The peppers are then drained, blended with high-quality all-natural vinegar, and stirred for several weeks. Finally the sauce is strained,

The Tabasco sauce factory on Avery Island, built in 1980.

bottled, and sent out across America and the world.

In south Louisiana we are well known for many things —swamps and bayous, alligators and muskrat, jazz and Bourbon Street, politics and preachers, Mardi Gras and Cajun fais-do-do dances, and most of all good food. We take great pleasure in both the preparation and enjoyment of our unique cuisine, an integral part of our culture. Many of our local specialties are neither low in fat nor quick and easy to prepare, but they are awfully good.

Here we've included what we believe to be the best of these recipes. Additionally, we give you favorite dishes collected over the years from many sources, including friends such as James Beard, Craig Claiborne, Pierre Franey, and Jeff Smith. In most recipes Tabasco pepper sauce is used as a flavor enhancer. If you want your food spicier, add more pepper sauce while making the dish or sprinkle it on at the table. We hope you will enjoy this collection and urge you to send us your favorite recipes— especially those that might call for a well-known brand of pepper sauce made on Avery Island.

PIQUANCY SCALE

By piquancy we mean an agreeable pungency or stimulation of the palate, not just heat or bite. The tiny Tabasco sauce bottles numbering from one to four, which appear at the top of each recipe, are intended only as guides to the level of piquancy in the dish. Tabasco sauce actually rounds out and enhances other flavors, contributing complexity and high notes where other pepper sauces only add heat. Even a recipe with a "four-bottle" rating won't blow you away, so if you like food very spicy, add more Tabasco sauce to your own taste. Remember, the perceived degree of heat in food is very subjective; what is hot to one person may be mild to another.

▮ = gives flavors a lift		▮▮▮ = definite authority	
▮▮ = a touch of heat		▮▮▮▮ = not for the meek	

A street in New Orleans' Vieux Carre is adorned with beautifully wrought iron of a Spanish pattern.

Soups &
Starters

PEPPERED PECANS

||||

A Louisiana tradition, these spicy pecans are eagerly anticipated by friends visiting our home during the holidays. The slow roasting in a low oven gives them extra crispness. They make a real nice gift, too.

3 tablespoons butter or margarine
3 cloves garlic, minced
2½ teaspoons Tabasco pepper sauce
½ teaspoon salt
3 cups pecan halves

Preheat the oven to 250° F.

In a small skillet, melt the butter over medium heat. Add the garlic, Tabasco sauce, and salt, and cook for a minute. Toss the pecans with the butter mixture and spread the nuts in a single layer on a baking sheet. Stirring occasionally, bake for 1 hour, or until the pecans are crisp.

When making popcorn, shake some Tabasco sauce into the cooking oil before adding the kernels for popcorn with zing.

•

MAKES 3 CUPS

ROASTED RED PEPPER DIP

A pleasant change from guacamole, this dip has the color and taste to complement crudités, toasted pita bread triangles, or crisp crackers.

2 red bell peppers
3 slices white bread, crusts removed
¼ cup milk
¼ cup pitted green olives
1 garlic clove
2 tablespoons olive oil
1 tablespoon fresh lemon juice
½ teaspoon Tabasco pepper sauce
Sliced green olives for garnish

Preheat the broiler. Slice the peppers in half lengthwise, and core and seed. Lay the pieces skin side up in a shallow broiling pan and set the pan 3 inches below the heat. Broil the peppers until the skin blisters and turns black. Remove the peppers to a plastic bag and close it; let them steam for 15 minutes. When they are cool enough to handle, peel off the skin. Meanwhile, break the bread into a small bowl, add the milk, and soak for 10 minutes.

Combine the bread, peppers, olives, and garlic in a food processor and process with a pulsing motion for about 4 seconds. Add the oil, lemon juice, and Tabasco sauce, and pulse 3 seconds longer. Spoon the dip into a serving bowl, cover, and let stand at least 30 minutes to blend the flavors. Garnish with sliced olives.

MAKES 1 ¼ CUPS

GUACAMOLE

III

If you're in a hurry and don't mind a smooth-textured guacamole, make this in a food processor, chopping the onion first and then adding the rest of the ingredients. By using Tabasco sauce, there's no need to handle hot peppers and the degree of hotness can easily be controlled.

2 ripe avocados, halved and pitted
1 small onion, finely chopped
2 tablespoons fresh lime or lemon juice
½ teaspoon Tabasco pepper sauce
½ teaspoon salt

With a spoon scoop the avocados into a medium bowl and mash them with a fork. Add the onion, lime or lemon juice, Tabasco sauce, and salt and blend gently but thoroughly. Cover and refrigerate for no more than an hour or so before serving. Serve with tortilla chips or crudités.

Combine 1 cup mayonnaise, 1 tablespoon ketchup, and 1 teaspoon Tabasco sauce and blend well for a perky crudité dip.

•

MAKES ABOUT 2 CUPS

MTK's SAUCED SHRIMP

▮▮▮

Martha Tupper Kay, a special lady from Mississippi, created recipes for McIlhenny Company for many years. She was famous for her shrimp sauce, which has a deliciously complex mix of condiments and spices. If you prefer, the sauce can be served on the side, for dipping.

½	cup sour cream
¼	cup mayonnaise
2	tablespoons chili sauce or tomato sauce
1	tablespoon fresh lemon juice
1	tablespoon drained horseradish
1½	teaspoons Worcestershire sauce
½	teaspoon Tabasco pepper sauce
1½	teaspoons curry powder
1	tablespoon finely minced mango chutney
2	tablespoons drained capers
2	pounds shrimp, cooked and shelled and deveined
1	tablespoon chopped fresh parsley

In large bowl stir together the sour cream, mayonnaise, chili sauce, lemon juice, horseradish, Worcestershire sauce, Tabasco sauce, curry powder, chutney, and capers. Pour the sauce over the shrimp and toss to coat. Refrigerate for several hours. To serve, mound the shrimp in a serving dish and sprinkle with the parsley and additional capers, if desired.

MAKES 12 HORS D'OEUVRES SERVINGS

CORNMEAL NIPS

♦♦♦

For a change of pace from crackers or rolls, serve these zesty little wafers with soups or salads.

   1 **cup yellow stone-ground cornmeal**
1½ **teaspoons sugar**
   1 **teaspoon salt**
   1 **teaspoon grated onion**
   2 **tablespoons butter or margarine**
   1 **teaspoon Tabasco pepper sauce**
1½ **cups boiling water**
   1 **large egg, lightly beaten**

Preheat the oven to 400° F. In a large bowl, mix together the cornmeal, sugar, salt, onion, butter, and Tabasco sauce. Add the boiling water and stir until it is absorbed. Stir in the egg. Drop by teaspoons onto a greased baking sheet. Bake for 15 minutes, then remove and cool on a rack.

Blend up to ½ teaspoon of Tabasco sauce into one half cup of softened butter and perk up steamed vegetables, breads—just about anything!

MAKES 4 DOZEN

EGGPLANT NEW IBERIA

‖‖

Eggplant is a favorite in Louisiana, where we fry it, smother it, devil it, bake it, and stuff it. This versatile recipe makes a delicious dip or spread.

1 medium eggplant
2 medium tomatoes, peeled, seeded, and diced (about 1 cup)
1 small garlic clove, minced
¾ cup chopped green onions
¼ cup chopped fresh parsley
5 tablespoons red wine vinegar
3 tablespoons olive oil
1 teaspoon ground cumin
¾ teaspoon Tabasco pepper sauce
½ teaspoon salt

Preheat the oven to 375° F. Trim the ends off the eggplant and cut the eggplant in half lengthwise. Placed the halves on a greased baking sheet, cut side down. Bake for 35 minutes, or until tender, then cool and peel and dice.

In a large bowl, mix the eggplant, tomatoes, garlic, green onions, and parsley. In a small bowl, stir together the remaining ingredients. Pour the marinade over the vegetables and mix well. Cover and let stand for several hours to blend the flavors. Serve at room temperature.

MAKES 1 QUART

NOTE: To microwave the eggplant instead of baking it, place the halves cut side down on a greased microwave-safe dish. Cook on high 5 to 6 minutes, or until tender.

FIERY
CATFISH FINGERS
IIII

In the South we grow up loving catfish, which is plentiful in the bayous and rivers. Now it's farm-grown, and northerners are discovering its mild and versatile flavor. We coat bite-size fingers of catfish fillets with plenty of Tabasco sauce and deep-fry them for a knock-your-socks-off appetizer.

> 1 cup yellow or coarse-ground mustard, or a combination of both
> 1 egg white, lightly beaten
> 2 teaspoons Tabasco pepper sauce
> 1½ pounds catfish fillets, cut into bite-size strips
> ½ cup yellow cornmeal
> ½ cup all-purpose flour
> ½ teaspoon salt
> ¼ teaspoon freshly ground black pepper
> 1 quart vegetable oil

In a large bowl, stir together the mustard, egg white, and Tabasco sauce. Add the fish and toss to coat well. Cover and marinate for 1 hour.

In a shallow dish, mix together the cornmeal, flour, salt, and pepper. Pour the oil into a heavy 3-quart saucepan or deep-fryer, filling it no more than one-third full, and heat over medium heat to 350° F. Dredge the fish in the cornmeal mixture and shake off the excess. Carefully add the fish to the oil, a few pieces at a time. Cook for 2 minutes, or until golden brown and crispy. Drain on paper towels. Serve the catfish hot with spicy mayonnaise or picante sauce.

SERVES 6 TO 8

GREEN VEGETABLE PÂTÉ

This vegetable pâté has lively flavor and texture, but is surprisingly low in calories.

- 1   envelope unflavored gelatin
- ½   cup cold water
- 1   tablespoon butter or margarine
- ½   cup thinly sliced onion
- ½   pound mushrooms, cleaned and sliced
- 1   10-ounce package frozen cut green beans
- ½   cup walnuts
- ½   cup parsley leaves
- ¼   cup mayonnaise
- 1   tablespoon fresh lemon juice
- 2   teaspoons Worcestershire sauce
- ¾   teaspoon salt
- ½   teaspoon Tabasco pepper sauce
- ¼   teaspoon dried fines herbes or herbes de Provence
- ⅛   teaspoon ground nutmeg

In a small saucepan, sprinkle the gelatin over the water. Place over low heat and stir constantly until the gelatin dissolves, about 3 minutes. Set aside.

In a large skillet, melt the butter, then add the onion and mushrooms and cook over medium heat for about 4 minutes. Add the beans, cover, and cook 4 to 5 minutes.

Put the cooked vegetables in the bowl of a food processor. Add the gelatin and the remaining ingredients, and process until pureed. Pour into a 3-cup mold and chill until firm. Unmold and serve with crackers.

SERVES 8

Libretto by R. A. Barnet — Burlesque Opera of Tabasco — Music by G. W. Chadwick

The Hasty Pudding Club of Harvard University produced a Tabasco opera with John Avery McIlhenny's approval in 1893. He later bought the rights to the production and had it staged in New York City.

THE TABASCO SAUCE TEMPEST

From its beginning, the British have appreciated Tabasco sauce. In 1868 U.S. wholesale sent Tabasco sauce to England, and as early as 1872 Grandpère opened an office in London to handle the orders pouring in from Europe.

England's love affair with Tabasco sauce nearly came to an end in 1932. Members of Parliament, fond of French wines and Cuban cigars, were also partial to Tabasco pepper sauce, readily available in the House of Commons dining rooms. But when the British Government embarked on an isolationist "Buy British" campaign, Parliament, following suit, banned the purchase of Tabasco sauce.

The ensuing cries of protest from the MP's were dubbed "The Tabasco Tempest" by amused observers, but generally ignored by the Government. However, inevitably "Buy British" gave way to "Buy Tabasco," and the little bottles of red sauce happily reappeared on parliamentary tables.

THE TABASCO COOKBOOK

HONEY MUSTARD CHICKEN BITES

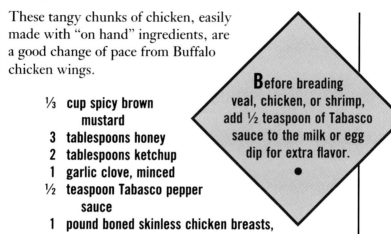

These tangy chunks of chicken, easily made with "on hand" ingredients, are a good change of pace from Buffalo chicken wings.

⅓ cup spicy brown mustard
3 tablespoons honey
2 tablespoons ketchup
1 garlic clove, minced
½ teaspoon Tabasco pepper sauce
1 pound boned skinless chicken breasts, cut into 1-inch pieces

Before breading veal, chicken, or shrimp, add ½ teaspoon of Tabasco sauce to the milk or egg dip for extra flavor.

In a medium bowl, mix the mustard, honey, ketchup, garlic, and Tabasco sauce. Set aside ¼ cup of the mixture; add the chicken to the rest and stir to coat. Cover and refrigerate for at least 1 hour, stirring occasionally.

Preheat the broiler. Arrange the chicken pieces on a rack in the broiler pan and broil, turning once and brushing with the marinade, until the chicken is tender, about 10 minutes. Serve with the reserved sauce as a dip.

SERVES 6

BAKED CHERRYSTONE CLAMS WITH SPICY BUTTER

||

When renowned chef Pierre Franey visited Avery Island, he observed some age-old local commercial enterprises—crawfish farming, oyster shucking, and boudin making—with great curiosity and enthusiasm. Here he brings his incomparable touch to cherrystone clams, best enjoyed with a loaf of crusty French bread and a carafe of wine. We southerners defer to the Yankees on this one.

36 cherrystone clams
1 cup (2 sticks) butter, at room temperature
¼ cup chopped shallots
1 tablespoon chopped garlic
½ teaspoon Tabasco pepper sauce
1 tablespoon Worcestershire sauce
1 tablespoon Dijon mustard
2 tablespoons chopped fresh parsley
2 tablespoons chopped fresh basil leaves
   Salt and freshly ground black pepper to taste

> **A** stick of butter melted with ¼ teaspoon Tabasco sauce makes a super dunk for lobster, clams, artichokes—anywhere plain butter is used.
>
> •

Preheat the broiler. Open the clams and arrange them neatly on half shells on a baking sheet. In a small bowl, cream the butter with the remaining ingredients. Spoon the mixture evenly over the clams. Place them under the broiler for 1 minute. Serve immediately with French bread.

SERVES 6 TO 8

HERBED SAUSAGES IN WINE

People line up for these at Point O'Woods on Fire Island, where they are a specialty at Barbara Hunter's parties. This recipe can easily be multiplied several times to serve a crowd.

½ pound Italian sweet sausage
½ pound Italian hot sausage
½ pound kielbasa
½ pound bockwurst (veal sausage)
5 green onions, minced
2 cups dry white wine
1 tablespoon chopped fresh basil leaves or
    ¼ teaspoon dried
1 teaspoon fresh thyme leaves or ¼ teaspoon dried
1 tablespoon finely chopped fresh parsley or
    1 teaspoon dried
½ teaspoon Tabasco pepper sauce

Cut the sausages into ½-inch pieces. In a deep skillet over medium heat, cook the Italian sausage for 3 to 5 minutes, or until lightly browned. Drain off the fat. Add the remaining sausage and the green onions, and cook for 5 minutes more. Reduce the heat to low, add the remaining ingredients, and simmer for 20 minutes, stirring occasionally. Serve immediately, or keep warm in a chafing dish. Serve with toothpicks.

MAKES 8 TO 10 SERVINGS

HOT 'N' SPICY CHICKEN WINGS
WITH BLUE CHEESE DIP

♦♦♦

Here's an easy version of the tangy chicken wings that have captivated people all over the country. To make them hotter, just use more Tabasco sauce. Serve these with plenty of napkins.

DIP
½ cup sour cream
½ cup mayonnaise
2 teaspoons white wine vinegar
1 tablespoon chopped fresh parsley
1 tablespoon chopped green onions
½ teaspoon minced garlic
½ teaspoon Tabasco pepper sauce
3 tablespoons crumbled blue cheese
Salt and freshly ground black pepper to taste

CHICKEN WINGS
12 chicken wings
Vegetable oil for frying
4 tablespoons melted butter or margarine
1 teaspoon ketchup
1 teaspoon Tabasco pepper sauce

Celery sticks

In a bowl, beat together all of the dip ingredients until blended. Set aside.

Remove the tips from the wings and discard. Separate the first and second joints of the wings with a sharp knife.

Pat the wings dry with paper towels. In a heavy saucepan, heat about 2 inches of oil to 350° F. on a deep-frying thermometer. Fry the wings, a few at a time, for about 6 minutes, until golden on all sides. Drain on paper towels.

In a small bowl, mix the butter, ketchup, and Tabasco sauce. Toss the wings in the butter mixture to coat thoroughly. Serve hot, and pass the dip and celery sticks.

MAKES 24 PIECES

A bottle carton stuffer from the early 1950s shows the myriad ways to use Tabasco sauce.

WHITE WINE GAZPACHO

In the South we serve cold soups frequently as a refreshing foil to the heat. Thin slices of zucchini and the piquancy of dry white wine plus Tabasco sauce give this gazpacho a delicious twist.

3   ripe tomatoes, peeled, cored, and seeded
1   tablespoon vegetable oil
1   cup thinly sliced green onions
1   cup thinly sliced zucchini cut into quarters
2   garlic cloves, minced
1   green or red pepper, cored, seeded, and cut
     into ½-inch strips
2   tablespoons chopped fresh parsley
½   teaspoon salt
½   teaspoon Tabasco pepper sauce
1½ cups chicken broth
⅓   cup dry white wine

Coarsely chop the tomatoes; you should have about 1¼ cups. Drain, reserving the liquid (about ½ cup). In a large skillet, heat the oil over medium heat. Add the green onions, zucchini, and garlic, and sauté for 1 minute. Add the tomatoes, pepper, parsley, salt, and Tabasco sauce. Stirring frequently, cook for 5 minutes, or until the pepper is tender. Turn the vegetables into a large bowl and mix in the reserved tomato liquid and the broth and wine. Cover and refrigerate for several hours or overnight.

SERVES 4

HOST PAR EXCELLENCE

An active member of the exclusive Chevaliers du Tastevin, Walter McIlhenny loved to entertain and dine well, carrying on the tradition started by Grandpère. He assembled a formidable cookbook collection, and counted among his many friends culinary greats such as Clementine Paddleford, James Beard, and Craig Claiborne. His kitchen was a large square room with a huge, six-by-nine-foot butcher block table dead center, and an array of gleaming copper pots hanging overhead. At his own choosing, his dining table seated no more than eight, so each guest could participate in the dinner conversation, and he personally selected the menu and the wines.

Although he built a new pepper sauce plant, introduced modern management and marketing, and expanded sales to over a hundred countries worldwide, Walter resisted pressure to sell the company or change the method of making the sauce. He retained the lengthy quality-minded process from the old family recipe, with its three-year aging. He always went into the pepper fields to weigh the day's harvest, and personally checked each barrel of aged pepper mash for aroma and color, as well as each batch of finished sauce—a tradition we carry on to this day.

BUTTERMILK BEET SOUP

Cousin Walter and those who dined with him looked forward to this well-chilled light beet soup on warm days. Milk, plain yogurt, or a combination of the two can be used instead of buttermilk.

          1   tablespoon butter
          1   cup finely chopped onion
         ¼   cup finely chopped celery
         ¼   cup chopped celery leaves
          3   cups peeled beets cut into julienne
          2   cups chicken broth
         ½   teaspoon Tabasco pepper sauce
         ¼   teaspoon salt
               Freshly ground black pepper to taste
        1½   teaspoons sugar
        1½   cups buttermilk
          2   teaspoons chopped fresh dill

Melt the butter in a medium saucepan. Add the onion and celery, and sauté over medium heat for 10 minutes, or until the onion is soft and golden. Add the celery leaves and cook for 2 minutes longer. Add the remaining ingredients except the buttermilk and dill. Bring to a boil, lower the heat, and simmer for 20 minutes, or until the beets are tender. Cool. Stir in the buttermilk and dill. Chill thoroughly.

SERVES 6

ZUCCHINI-CRESS SOUP

I generally like zucchini raw on a vegetable tray or cooked in ratatouille. But here's a wonderful zucchini soup that gives welcome relief in our hot and humid Louisiana summers. It's a velvety-smooth soup with no cream, so it's easy on the calories, but it tastes like an indulgence.

1 tablespoon butter or margarine
½ cup sliced onion
2 cups chicken broth
2 cups diced unpeeled zucchini
½ cup watercress leaves, washed
½ cup peeled and chopped potato
3 parsley sprigs
½ teaspoon Tabasco pepper sauce
Plain yogurt or sour cream

In a medium saucepan, melt the butter and sauté the onion until tender, about 2 minutes. Add the broth, zucchini, watercress, potato, parsley, and Tabasco sauce, and stir well. Bring to a boil, then reduce the heat, cover, and simmer for 20 minutes, until the potato is soft. Cool. Puree the soup in two batches in a blender or food processor. Chill. Serve with yogurt or sour cream.

SERVES 4

SOUPED-UP SOUPS

Other soups that get a lift from Tabasco sauce with just a half teaspoon or so for 4 servings are vichyssoise and other potato soups, borscht, clam chowder, beef consommé, shrimp bisque, chicken soup, crab soup, and onion, pea, bean, lentil, and other vegetable soups.

POTATO, ARTICHOKE AND LEEK SOUP

"Elegant" describes this simple creamy soup of leeks, potatoes, and artichoke hearts, sparked with Tabasco pepper sauce. It is superb served in hollowed-out boule bread.

- 2 tablespoons butter or margarine
- ½ cup chopped onion
- 1½ cups cleaned and chopped leeks, white and light green parts only
- 1 teaspoon minced garlic
- 1 quart chicken broth
- 1 13¾-ounce can artichoke hearts, well rinsed and drained, quartered
- 2½ cups peeled and cubed baking potatoes
- 2 small thyme sprigs
- 1½ cups milk
- ¾ teaspoon Tabasco pepper sauce
  Salt and freshly ground black pepper to taste
  Chopped fresh parsley

In a medium saucepan, melt the butter and sauté the onion and leeks, covered, for about 10 minutes, or until tender. Uncover and cook until the leeks are very soft, about 5 minutes, adding the garlic for the last minute. Add the broth, artichokes, potatoes, and thyme, and simmer for 15 minutes, or until the potatoes are tender. Add the milk and Tabasco sauce, and simmer for 5 minutes longer. Remove from the heat and discard the thyme. In a food processor or blender, puree the soup until very smooth. Add salt and pepper to taste. Serve hot or cold, garnished with parsley.

SERVES 8 TO 10

OYSTER BISQUE

‖

Chilled Louisiana raw oysters and Tabasco sauce
go together like caviar and champagne. Oysters are great
in cooked dishes, too, such as our satisfying bisque.

1 dozen (1 pint) shucked large raw
  oysters, 1 cup liquor reserved
4 cups milk
1 thick onion slice
2 celery stalks, cut into
  pieces
1 parsley sprig
1 bay leaf
4 tablespoons melted butter
¼ cup all-purpose flour
½ teaspoon salt
¾ teaspoon Tabasco pepper sauce
  Chopped chives

Add a finishing dash of Tabasco sauce to each bowl of oyster stew, clam chowder, or seafood bisque before serving.

Dice the oysters and put them in a saucepan with the
reserved liquor. Over medium-low heat, slowly bring the
oysters to a boil; remove from the heat. Scald the milk
with the onion, celery, parsley, and bay leaf, then strain
out the seasonings. In a large saucepan, blend the butter
with the flour, salt, and Tabasco sauce. Slowly stir in the
milk, and stir over low heat until thickened. Add the oysters and their liquor, and stir for 1 minute, until heated
through. Pour into serving bowls and sprinkle with chives.

S E R V E S 4

VERMILLION BAY FISH CHOWDER

TABASCO CLASSIC Our Bayou Petit Anse, surrounding a good bit of Avery Island, flows into Vermillion Bay, which in turn leads into the Gulf of Mexico. The waters of the bay are home to many species of fish, including the delicious flounder, but any white fish can be substituted in this excellent chowder.

    4   tablespoons butter or margarine
    ½   cup chopped celery
    ½   cup chopped onion
    ¼   cup all-purpose flour
    2   cups milk
    1   8-ounce bottle clam juice
    ½   teaspoon dried basil
    ½   teaspoon dried thyme
    ½   teaspoon salt
    ½   teaspoon Tabasco pepper sauce
    1   pound flounder fillets, cut into 1-inch pieces
    2   cups cubed peeled and cooked potatoes
    1   17-ounce can whole-kernel corn, undrained

In a 4-quart saucepan, melt the butter over medium heat. Add the celery and onion and cook for 5 minutes, or until tender, stirring frequently. Stir in the flour and cook for 3 minutes. Gradually stir in the milk and clam juice until smooth. Blend in the basil, thyme, salt, and Tabasco sauce. Gently stir in the fish, potatoes, and corn. Cook over low heat for 5 minutes, or until the fish flakes easily.

SERVES 6

BREAKFAST&
BRUNCH

RUDY'S CHEESE OMELETTES À LA SUDS

More than a decade ago, Rudy Stanish, "the Omelette King," would turn out hundreds of omelettes at a time for charity functions. He always added Tabasco pepper sauce to his egg mixture, and over the years he cooked a bunch of omelettes for us on many occasions. Rudy used beer as the liquid in this cheese omelette recipe, giving the eggs even more zip.

6   **large eggs**
⅓   **cup beer**
½   **teaspoon Tabasco pepper sauce**
3   **tablespoons butter**
3   **tablespoons grated Parmesan cheese**

In a large mixing bowl, beat the eggs, beer, and Tabasco sauce with a whisk only until blended, not frothy. In an 8½-inch omelette pan over medium heat, melt 1 tablespoon of the butter. The pan is hot enough when a drop of water spatters in it. Pour one-third of the egg mixture into the pan. Place one hand on the pan handle, palm down, and move the pan in a back-and-forth motion. With the other hand, using a fork, stir the egg mixture in a circular motion, about seven times. Sprinkle the omelette with a tablespoon of the cheese. To turn out the omelette, place your hand on the handle with palm upward. Tip the pan and roll the omelette out onto a plate. Repeat twice with the remaining egg mixture. Serve with additional Tabasco sauce, if desired.

SERVES 3

SHIRRED EGGS WITH SHERRIED MUSHROOMS

‖

One of Cousin Walter's breakfast favorites was shirred eggs with a rasher of bacon. The sherry in the mushrooms gives these eggs a delightfully different flavor, great for brunch accompanied by a spicy Bloody Mary.

4 tablespoons butter or margarine
¾ pound fresh mushrooms, cleaned and finely chopped
¾ cup finely chopped onion
1 tablespoon dry sherry
¾ teaspoon Tabasco pepper sauce
¼ teaspoon salt
4 thin slices French bread, toasted
8 eggs
Chopped fresh parsley

Preheat the oven to 350° F. In a large skillet, heat 2 tablespoons of the butter. Add the mushrooms and onion, and cook until tender, about 5 minutes. Stir in the sherry, Tabasco sauce, and salt, and cook for 1 minute longer. Spread the toast with the remaining 2 tablespoons butter. Grease 4 ramekins. Fit a slice of toast into each ramekin, and top with a layer of onions and mushrooms. Carefully break 2 eggs into each ramekin. Bake for 15 to 20 minutes, until the eggs are set. Sprinkle with parsley.

SERVES 4

PUFFED-UP OMELETTE

This is a spectacular way to serve eggs, the omelette emerging from the oven looking like a soufflé with a golden brown top. It truly makes four eggs eat deliciously like eight, a plus for those watching their cholesterol. For extra volume, add two more egg whites. A straight-sided cast-iron skillet is best for this, and, like a soufflé, a puffy omelette waits for no one.

¼ cup milk
4 egg yolks
½ teaspoon Tabasco pepper sauce
1 teaspoon double-acting baking powder
4 to 6 large egg whites
⅛ teaspoon salt
1 tablespoon butter or margarine
Chopped fresh parsley, snipped chives, or grated Parmesan cheese (optional)

Preheat the oven to 350° F. In a small bowl, beat the milk, egg yolks, Tabasco sauce, and baking powder with a fork. In a larger bowl, beat the egg whites with the salt until they are stiff but not dry. Fold the yolk mixture lightly into the whites. In a heavy ovenproof 10-inch skillet, melt the butter over low heat. Pour the egg mixture into the skillet. Cook the omelette over low heat, slashing it through with a knife to allow the heat to penetrate. When the omelette is half done (after about 5 minutes), place it on a rack in the oven and bake for about 10 minutes, or until the top is set and lightly browned. Serve at once, using two forks to divide the omelette into 4 wedges. Serve with a sprinkling of parsley, chives, or cheese, if desired.

SERVES 4

Eggs and Tabasco Sauce:
A Match Made in... Heaven?

Tabasco sauce and eggs are a natural. Even kids say eggs taste better with a drop or two of pepper sauce.

- For scrambled eggs and omelettes, add ¼ teaspoon Tabasco sauce for every 3 eggs.
- Sprinkle a drop or two of Tabasco on each coddled, shirred (baked), or poached egg.
- Give extra kick to your favorite deviled egg recipe by mixing ½ teaspoon of Tabasco sauce into the yolk mixture for a dozen eggs.
- Soufflés rise to new heights with the addition of at least ½ teaspoon Tabasco sauce per recipe.
- Quiches become extra special with ½ teaspoon Tabasco sauce mixed in.
- Dishes like huevos rancheros can take more—a teaspoon of Tabasco sauce for 8 eggs.

HERBED CHEESE TORTE

A wonderful brunch or supper dish, this creamy torte is simple to put together with a food processor and is so good people always want a second helping.

    4   cups (2 pounds) creamed cottage cheese
        Pastry for a two-crust pie
    1   small onion, coarsely chopped
    ¾   cup fresh parsley leaves
    ½   cup freshly grated Parmesan cheese
    3   tablespoons flour
    1   teaspoon fresh lemon juice
    ¾   teaspoon salt
    ¾   teaspoon Tabasco pepper sauce
    ½   teaspoon crumbled dried oregano
    ½   teaspoon dried chervil
    4   large eggs
        Tomato wedges for garnish

Put the cottage cheese in a colander over a large bowl and cover. Drain overnight in the refrigerator. Discard the liquid.

Preheat the oven to 450° F. Line the bottom of a 9-inch springform pan with half of the pastry, and prick it with a fork. Bake the pastry for 8 minutes. Remove and cool. Lower the oven temperature to 400° F. Press the remaining pastry around the sides of the pan.

In a food processor, combine the cottage cheese, onion, parsley, Parmesan, flour, lemon juice, salt, Tabasco sauce, oregano, and chervil, and process until smooth. With the motor running, drop in the eggs, one at a time, and process for 30 seconds longer. Pour the mixture into the pan.

Bake the torte for 10 minutes, then reduce the heat to 325° F. and bake for 50 minutes longer, or until the tip of a knife inserted in the center comes out clean. Let it stand 15 minutes before serving. Garnish with tomato wedges.

SERVES 10 TO 12

TABASCO SAUCE LOVES CHEESE

Tabasco sauce sparks up cheeses of all kinds, bland or sharp. Stir a few drops into cottage cheese and cream cheese dips and spreads, sprinkle it on grilled cheese sandwiches or cheese straws, shake it into fondue, rarebit, quiche, macaroni and cheese, cheese bread, soufflés, cheese balls, cheese soup ... even add a dash to raclette.

For more than a hundred years, a member of the McIlhenny family has weighed the peppers after each harvest, as Paul is doing here in the mid-1970s.

CHICKEN HASH

Despite its plebeian name, this superb dish is right at home on an elegant table. Here's our version, which is an exceptional way to use up leftover roast chicken.

VELOUTÉ SAUCE
- 3 tablespoons butter
- 1½ cups half-and-half
- ½ cup chicken broth
- 3 tablespoons flour
- ½ teaspoon Tabasco pepper sauce
- Salt and freshly ground black pepper to taste

HASH
- 2 tablespoons butter
- ½ cup finely chopped onion
- ½ cup finely chopped red or yellow pepper
- 6 ounces mushrooms, cleaned and thinly sliced
- 2 tablespoons chopped fresh parsley
- Salt and freshly ground black pepper to taste
- 2 cups diced cooked peeled potatoes
- 2 cups diced cooked chicken

Chopped chives

For the sauce, melt the butter in a small saucepan; warm the half-and-half and broth in a separate pan. When the butter foams, sprinkle in the flour and cook, stirring, over low heat for 3 minutes. Add the broth mixture, Tabasco sauce, and salt and pepper. Cook, stirring, for about 2 minutes, or until the sauce thickens. Set aside.

Preheat the oven to 400° F. In a medium skillet, heat the butter and add the onion and red pepper. Cook over medium heat until tender, then add the mushrooms, pars-

Edmund McIlhenny's wife, Mary Eliza Avery McIlhenny, otherwise known as Grandmere. The two were married in 1859.

ley, and salt and pepper. Cook over medium-low heat until all the vegetables are very tender, about 15 minutes. Combine with the sauce, potatoes, and chicken, and turn into a buttered shallow baking dish. Bake on the top oven rack for 30 to 40 minutes, or until the hash is bubbling and the top is golden. Sprinkle with chives before serving.

SERVES 4 TO 6

GRILLADES FOR BRUNCH

⫶

Grillades are a southern breakfast specialty that always meets an enthusiastic reception at our breakfast table, served with a light, flavorful grits pudding or spoon bread. Grillades should be simmered long enough to be fork-tender, refrigerated overnight, and reheated in the morning. Make them with beef or veal, or try venison, which I cut into julienne-size strips.

2	pounds veal or beef, ½″ thick, trimmed and cut into small serving pieces
¼	cup vegetable oil
¼	cup all-purpose flour
1	cup chopped onion
1½	cups chopped green pepper
2	garlic cloves, minced
1	cup chopped fresh tomatoes
½	teaspoon dried thyme
¾	cup beef broth
½	cup red wine
¾	teaspoon salt
1	bay leaf
2	teaspoons Tabasco pepper sauce
1	tablespoon Worcestershire sauce
3	tablespoons chopped fresh parsley

Pound the pieces of meat to ¼ inch thick. In a Dutch oven or heavy pot heat 2 tablespoons of the oil and brown the meat well in batches, removing each batch to a warm plate. Add the remaining 2 tablespoons oil and the flour to the pot. Stir over medium heat for about 30 minutes to make a dark brown roux.

Add the onion, green pepper, and garlic, and sauté for about 5 minutes, until soft, stirring often. Add the tomatoes and thyme, and cook, stirring, for 3 minutes. Add the broth and wine. Stir well for several minutes, scraping up bits from the bottom of pan. Return the meat to the pot and stir in the salt, bay leaf, Tabasco sauce, and Worcestershire sauce. Lower the heat and simmer, covered, for 1½ hours, or until the meat is very tender, stirring occasionally.

Remove the bay leaf. Stir in the parsley, cool, and refrigerate overnight. Reheat the grillades before serving, and serve with Cheese Grits (page 48).

SERVES 6 TO 8

TABASCO SAUCE AT BREAKFAST

Tabasco sauce really wakes up the taste buds. Try it in your favorite pancake batter, whip it into scrambled eggs, stir it into grits, sprinkle it on sausages, shake it on fried or poached eggs. For Hotovers, add ½ teaspoon Tabasco sauce with the milk called for in your favorite popover recipe or mix.

CHEESE GRITS

II

No Tabasco sauce cookbook would be complete without a recipe for grits. This one has lots of flavor, so it stands up to our famous grillades, and also works nicely with the gravy of any game or chicken dish.

- 4 **cups chicken broth**
- 1 **cup quick-cooking grits**
- 1½ **cups shredded sharp cheddar cheese**
- 1 **cup milk**
- 2 **large eggs, beaten**
- ¾ **teaspoon Tabasco pepper sauce**

Preheat the oven to 350° F. In a medium saucepan, bring the broth to a boil. Add the grits and cook according to package directions. Remove from the heat and stir in the cheese. In a bowl, combine the milk, eggs, and Tabasco sauce, then stir into the grits. Pour the grits into a lightly greased casserole and bake for 30 minutes. Serve with Grillades (pages 46–47).

SERVES 6 TO 8

PRESIDENTIAL SEAL
OF APPROVAL

From at least as early as John Avery McIlhenny's association with President Theodore Roosevelt, Tabasco sauce often has been a favorite of heads of state and other notables. For example, Britain's Queen Mother prefers it in her lobster cocktail.

In the 1960s, after one of President Kennedy's weekly White House breakfasts for congressional leaders, House Majority Whip Hale Boggs lamented, "We had serious problems—at breakfast there were no grits, no chicory in the coffee, and no Tabasco sauce!"

When George Bush campaigned in 1988, it was predicted that Tabasco sauce would replace jelly beans as the presidential favorite. A campaign spokesperson characterized Mr. Bush as "a devotee of Tabasco sauce. He uses Tabasco on his tuna sandwiches and on his eggs." His aides revealed that Mr. Bush ordered bottles sent to his hotel room in advance of every campaign stop. His favorite snack was reported to be fried pork rinds sprinkled with Tabasco sauce. After he received the GOP nomination in New Orleans, Mr. Bush handed out personalized bottles of our pepper sauce as presents for members of his family who dined with him at Arnaud's Restaurant. I wonder if he first started using it in Milton, Massachusetts, or Houston, Texas.

FRESH CORN PUDDING

||

TABASCO CLASSIC This simple but delicious fresh corn custard gets a boost from a lacing of Tabasco sauce and a sprinkling of paprika.

　　2　cups milk
　　1　tablespoon butter or margarine
　　3　large eggs
　¼　cup all-purpose flour
　¾　teaspoon salt
　　1　teaspoon Tabasco pepper sauce
　　2　cups fresh corn kernels, cut from the cob
　¾　cup coarsely chopped red or green bell pepper
　　　Paprika

Preheat the oven to 325° F. In a small saucepan scald the milk, then stir in the butter, and remove from the heat.

In a small mixing bowl whisk the eggs until foamy, then beat in the flour, salt, and Tabasco sauce. Gradually beat in the milk mixture. Add the corn and bell pepper and mix well. Pour the mixture into a buttered 2-quart baking dish and sprinkle the top generously with paprika. Set the dish in a larger pan, then add hot water to the larger pan until it is filled 3 inches deep. Bake for 1 hour and 15 minutes, or until the point of a knife inserted in the center of the pudding comes out clean. Let the pudding stand for 10 minutes before serving.

SERVES 4

CLASSIC BLOODY MARY

The Bloody Mary was created during the 1920s by Fernand Petiot, an American working at Harry's Bar in Paris. Tabasco sauce was added in the 1930s, when the drink was first served at the King Cole Bar in New York's St. Regis Hotel to please patrons who wanted a spicier drink. Variations of the Bloody Mary are countless, using ingredients such as clam juice, beef broth, horseradish, garlic, cumin, fresh herbs, coriander, curry powder, soy sauce, barbecue sauce, tequila, aquavit, and even sake.

Add three drops of Tabasco sauce to each serving of tomato or vegetable juice, or add ¼ teaspoon to each quart.

- 1 quart tomato juice
- 1 cup vodka or gin
- 1 tablespoon fresh lime or lemon juice
- 1 tablespoon Worcestershire sauce
- 1 teaspoon salt
- ¼ teaspoon Tabasco pepper sauce, or to taste

Combine all of the ingredients in a 2-quart pitcher. Stir well and refrigerate until chilled. Serve over ice, garnished with lime slices, celery stalks, or Zydeco Green Beans (page 119). For a spicier drink, add more Tabasco sauce.

SERVES 6

SANGRITA

‖

This is a drink with spirit—an interesting alternative to the usual brunch offering.

  1 small onion, peeled and quartered
  1 cup fresh orange juice
  4 cups tomato juice
 ⅓ cup fresh lime juice
  2 tablespoons fresh lemon juice
  1 teaspoon Worcestershire sauce
  1 teaspoon sugar
 ¾ teaspoon Tabasco pepper sauce
1¼ cups tequila

For a real kick, create a Cola Volcano by stirring in a drop or two of Tabasco sauce to a cola drink and serving it poured over ice.

In a blender, combine the onion and orange juice and process until smooth. Pour into a 3-quart pitcher. Add the tomato juice, lime juice, lemon juice, Worcestershire sauce, sugar, and Tabasco sauce. Mix well. Add the tequila and stir. Serve over ice, garnished with lime, lemon, and orange slices.

SERVES 10

ENTRÉES

—·—

EULA MAE'S CAJUN SEAFOOD GUMBO

┃┃

TABASCO CLASSIC Eula Mae Dore is a legend on Avery Island. She recently retired as proprietor of our Tabasco deli, where she served wonderful sandwiches and salads to the workers who dropped in for lunch. She and I have a standing dispute about the proper way to cook seafood gumbo. She insists on Cajun style, which is *never* made with a roux, while I grew up with the New Orleans roux-based version. Although I disagree with her method, the result is undeniably delicious.

¾ cup vegetable oil
2 pounds fresh okra or 2 16-ounce packages frozen okra, thawed, thinly sliced (about 8 cups)
1 tablespoon white vinegar
4 quarts water
2 pounds cubed cooked ham
3 large onions, diced
2 stalks celery, diced
1 head garlic, cloves peeled but left whole
1 green pepper, cored, seeded, and diced
1 16-ounce can whole tomatoes, drained and chopped
4 pounds medium shrimp, shelled and deveined
2 pounds lump crab meat
2 teaspoons Tabasco pepper sauce
6 cups cooked rice

Heat ½ cup of the oil in a large skillet (not cast iron) over medium heat and add the okra. Cook, stirring frequently, until it is no longer ropy, about 30 minutes. Add the vinegar and cook, stirring, for another 10 minutes, until the okra takes on a brownish color and is reduced to about

Eula Mae Dore often cooks her wonderful Cajun specialties
for guests at Marsh House, the original family homestead.

a quarter of its original volume. Put the okra in a medium
bowl and set aside.

In a large stockpot over high heat, bring the water to a
boil. Meanwhile, add the remaining ¼ cup oil and the
ham to the skillet. Sauté the ham over medium-high heat
for about 10 minutes, or until it is lightly browned. With
a slotted spoon, remove the ham to the stockpot. In the
same skillet, combine the onions, celery, garlic, and pepper, and cook, stirring constantly, for 10 minutes, until
the vegetables are tender. Add the vegetables, okra, and
tomatoes to the stockpot; cover and simmer over medium
heat for 1 hour.

Reduce the heat to very low, add the shrimp, and sim-
mer very slowly for 10 minutes. Add the crab meat and
Tabasco sauce; simmer for an additional 5 to 10 minutes.
Serve the gumbo in soup bowls with scoops of rice.

S ERVES 12 TO 16

CHICKEN AND ANDOUILLE GUMBO

||

TABASCO CLASSIC If you asked a dozen Louisiana cooks for their gumbo recipes you would get a dozen different ones— providing they agreed to part with their closely guarded family secrets. Gumbos are categorized in many ways: those made with a roux, without a roux, with okra, without okra, with filé, etc. There is seafood gumbo, oyster gumbo, gumbo z'herbes, chicken and sausage gumbo, and various combinations thereof. Here is a meat-based version with a full, rich flavor.

½ pound andouille or kielbasa sausage, cut into
   ¼-inch cubes
4 tablespoons vegetable oil
1 2½- to 3-pound chicken, cut into pieces
1½ quarts water
⅓ cup all-purpose flour
1 cup chopped onion
1 cup chopped celery
1 cup chopped green pepper
2 garlic cloves, minced
2 tablespoons chopped fresh parsley
2 bay leaves
½ teaspoon dried thyme
1 teaspoon Tabasco pepper sauce
¼ teaspoon salt
⅛ teaspoon freshly ground black pepper
½ cup chopped green onions
   Cooked rice

In a 3-quart saucepan over medium-high heat, brown the sausage in 2 tablespoons of the oil, about 7 minutes. Remove with a slotted spoon and set aside. Add the chicken pieces and cook until golden brown, about 10 minutes, turning occasionally. Add the water, cover, and cook until the chicken is tender, about 30 minutes. Remove the chicken, leaving the liquid in the pan, and when the chicken is cool enough to handle, discard the skin and bones and dice the meat into ½-inch cubes.

In a skillet over medium heat, mix the remaining 2 tablespoons oil and the flour and cook, stirring constantly, until the roux turns dark brown, about 30 minutes. Add the onion, celery, green pepper, garlic, and parsley, and cook for about 10 minutes, or until the vegetables are tender. Add the vegetables to the liquid in the saucepan, along with the bay leaf, thyme, Tabasco sauce, salt, and pepper. Bring to a boil, reduce the heat, and simmer, uncovered, for 45 minutes. Add the chicken and sausage and simmer for another 15 minutes.

Remove the pan from the heat, add the green onions, and adjust the seasoning. Let the gumbo stand for 10 to 15 minutes. To serve, mound about ⅓ cup rice in each soup bowl, then ladle about 1 cup of gumbo around the rice.

SERVES 6 TO 8

GUMBO

Gumbo is a classic Creole or Cajun hearty soup or stew, thickened with okra or filé, and served with steamed white rice. If okra is used, it is first cooked in a skillet with a little oil for 30 to 40 minutes, until it loses its slimy ropiness and browns slightly. A teaspoon of vinegar added toward the end of the cooking period helps get rid of the ropiness.

Filé, actually dried and ground young sassafras leaves, originally came from the Choctaw Indians. *Filé* means "to make threads," and that's what it does when added at the beginning of the cooking process. It should not boil.

Gumbo is a super way to use leftovers or to combine several meats in a single dish, such as chicken or duck with ham or sausages or a combination of seafood, like shrimp, oysters, and crab. No two gumbos are alike, and they are as good as the cook who makes them.

FRED'S HOTTEST SHRIMP

▮▮▮▮

Fred Ferretti, who writes a regular column in *Gourmet* magazine, is rumored to carry a flask of Tabasco sauce on his hip. He insists this is an exaggeration, but he has been known to shake droplets of the pepper sauce even on dim sum. Here's his recipe for shrimp with a real kick.

1   pound medium shrimp (about 36), shelled and deveined, shells reserved
½   cup water
2   teaspoons Tabasco pepper sauce
1   tablespoon ketchup
1   teaspoon salt
1½ teaspoons sugar
     Pinch of white pepper
4   tablespoons olive oil
1   small green pepper, cut into ½-inch cubes
1   small red pepper, cut into ½-inch cubes
4   garlic cloves, minced
½   cup diced onion
1   tablespoon white wine

In a small saucepan, combine the shrimp shells with the water and boil for 10 minutes. Remove the shells and reserve the stock. In a small bowl, combine 1 tablespoon of the shrimp stock with the Tabasco sauce, ketchup, salt, and sugar; set aside. Heat 1½ tablespoons of oil in a large skillet over high heat. When the oil is hot, add the bell peppers and sauté for 1 minute, then remove the peppers and set aside. Wipe the pan clean and add the remaining 2½ tablespoons oil and the garlic and onion. Cook over high heat for about 4 minutes, or until the onion is softened and translucent. Stir in the shrimp and cook for 1 minute. Add the wine and mix well. The shrimp should begin to curl. Add the reserved peppers and stir, cooking for about 30 seconds. Stir the Tabasco sauce mixture and pour it into the skillet, mixing all ingredients thoroughly. Remove the pan from the heat and transfer the shrimp with the sauce to a warmed serving dish. Serve immediately with cooked rice.

SERVES 4

ROUX
—•—

Roux, a mixture of flour and oil or drippings browned slowly over medium heat until the desired color is achieved, is a basic component of Louisiana cooking. It is the starter for many fine Cajun and Creole dishes, such as gumbo, oyster pie, crawfish bisque, oyster stew, turtle soup, étouffée, grillades, etc., contributing color, body, and often a nutty flavor.

To make a roux, melt equal amounts of butter (or oil, shortening, or bacon drippings) and flour in a heavy pot or skillet over medium heat. Stir constantly until the mixture reaches a golden or deeper brown, taking care not to burn the mixture. This can take 20 minutes or more, depending upon the desired darkness of the roux. Don't hurry it. If the mixture burns, discard it and begin again, because even slightly burned roux will ruin a dish. A good rule of thumb is to make the roux one shade darker than you want the finished dish.

A quick-and-dirty roux can be made in the microwave. In a microwave-safe dish, combine ½ cup each of flour and oil. Cover and cook on high for 2 to 3 minutes. Stir the mixture and continue cooking, stirring after each minute, until it reaches the proper color.

SHRIMP CREOLE

II

We love this New Orleans classic spooned over rice, served with crusty bread and a green salad. This is the version we offer to guests, especially those from other areas, as an example of our fine regional cooking. At least a tablespoon of bacon drippings is needed for flavor.

¼ cup all-purpose flour
1 tablespoon bacon drippings
3 tablespoons vegetable oil
2 cups chopped onion
½ cup chopped green onions
2 garlic cloves, minced
1 cup chopped green pepper
1 cup chopped celery, with leaves
1 teaspoon dried thyme
2 bay leaves
2 teaspoons salt
½ teaspoon freshly ground black pepper
1 6-ounce can tomato paste
1 16-ounce can tomatoes
1 8-ounce can tomato sauce
1 cup fish stock or water
4 pounds medium shrimp, shelled and deveined
1 teaspoon Tabasco pepper sauce
½ cup chopped fresh parsley
1 tablespoon fresh lemon juice
2 cups cooked rice

In a Dutch oven or large, heavy pan over medium heat, stir the flour, drippings, and oil until the roux becomes a deep red-brown, about 30 minutes. Add the onion, green onions, garlic, green pepper, celery, thyme, bay leaves, salt, and black pepper. Cook, stirring constantly, until the onion is transparent and soft, about 20 minutes. Add the tomato paste and cook for 3 minutes. Chop the tomatoes and add them, with their liquid, the tomato sauce, and the stock. Simmer, partially covered, for 1 hour, stirring occasionally.

Add the shrimp and cook until they are just done, about 5 minutes. Stir in the Tabasco sauce, parsley, and lemon juice. Cover and remove from the heat. This dish is best when allowed to stand several hours or overnight in the refrigerator. Reheat quickly, without boiling, and serve immediately over rice.

SERVES 8

CAPSICUM, A COLUMBUS DISCOVERY

Tabasco sauce is made from a variety of pepper called *Capsicum frutescens,* known for centuries in Latin America. The first written reference to a capsicum pepper was made in 1493 by Dr. Chauca, the physician on Columbus's voyage, who reported that the Indians used a spice called "agi," made from these peppers. Although his search for black pepper was fruitless, Columbus introduced capsicum peppers to the Old World.

A capsicum pepper's personality is determined by an alkaloid called capsaicin, an unusually powerful compound found in no other plant. Hotness in peppers ranges from the mildest bell peppers, with a zero score, to the habeneros, which rate 200,000 to 300,000 units on the Scoville scale, an organoleptic test devised in 1912 by a pharmacologist named Wilbur Scoville. The *Capsicum frutescens* variety has only a single cultivar in the United States, called variety tabasco, which has a high Scoville score. The varietal name of the pepper should not be confused with the trademark Tabasco ®.

SCALLOPS IN DOUBLE PEPPER SAUCE

||

Slivers of red and green bell peppers give this quickly prepared dish vibrant color, and the garlic, Tabasco sauce, and capers provide lots of flavor.

- ¼ cup olive oil
- 5 garlic cloves, coarsely chopped
- 1 pound bay or sea scallops
- ¾ cup slivered red peppers
- ¾ cup slivered green peppers
- ½ cup chopped onion
- ½ teaspoon Tabasco pepper sauce
- ¼ teaspoon salt
- 2 tablespoons drained capers

In a large skillet, heat the oil and add the garlic. Cook until golden, about 1 minute. Add the scallops, peppers, onion, Tabasco sauce, and salt. Stirring constantly, cook for 5 minutes, or until the scallops turn white and the vegetables are tender-crisp. Stir in the capers and serve immediately.

SERVES 4

TABASCO SAUCE AND SEAFOOD

Tabasco sauce is the perfect partner for all sorts of seafood. Sprinkle it on sautéed soft-shell crabs, pan-fried trout or shad roe, grilled fish, boiled crabs or shrimp, clam fritters, seviche, clams casino, and oysters Rockefeller. For more delicate-flavored fish and seafood, mix Tabasco sauce with melted butter or add it to cocktail sauce. The exception is oysters, which revel in the red stuff.

UNCLE NED SAVES
THE EGRETS

At the turn of the century my great-uncle Edward Avery McIlhenny, Grandpère's second son and a naturalist, returned from an Arctic expedition to find that the snowy egrets were almost gone from the Louisiana swamps, victims of the fashion of feathery aigrette plumes on ladies' hats. After searching for weeks, he found eight young egrets, which he took back to Avery Island and raised in a large cage, releasing them in the fall to migrate across the Gulf of Mexico. Six returned the next spring, forming the nucleus of a bird colony that now numbers in the tens of thousands. Over his life, Uncle Ned banded nearly two hundred thousand birds, crucial in mapping the North American migratory routes.

Uncle Ned succeeded Uncle John as president of the company. He was a visionary conservationist who persuaded the Rockefeller Foundation to give Louisiana 164,664 acres of marshland as wintering grounds for the millions of migratory waterfowl following the Mississippi flyway.

Uncle Ned created the beautiful Jungle Gardens on Avery Island, and when oil was discovered in 1942 he insisted that the integrity of the island's appearance and its role as a wildlife refuge be preserved. Live oak trees were bypassed, pipelines buried or painted green, and in this manner the natural beauty of the island was maintained.

OYSTER-ARTICHOKE PAN ROAST

❦

Each year McIlhenny Company sponsors a national Tabasco Community Cookbook Awards competition. The very first winner, in 1990, was *From a Lighthouse Window*, published by the Chesapeake Bay Maritime Museum in St. Michael's, Maryland. One of the standout recipes was this marvelous dish teaming oysters with artichokes.

  1 14-ounce can artichoke hearts in water, drained
        and quartered
  6 tablespoons butter or margarine
  1 cup chopped green onions
  ½ cup chopped onion
  1 garlic clove, minced
  3 tablespoons flour
  1 quart shucked oysters with their liquor
  ½ cup chopped fresh parsley
  1 teaspoon Worcestershire sauce
  1 tablespoon lemon juice
  ¼ teaspoon Tabasco pepper sauce
  ½ teaspoon salt
  1 cup fresh bread crumbs

In a small pan, cover the artichoke hearts with water and bring to a low simmer. Meanwhile, in a medium skillet heat 4 tablespoons of the butter and sauté the green onions, onion, and garlic until tender, about 3 minutes. Sprinkle on the flour and sauté, stirring, for another 3 minutes. While the vegetables are cooking, bring the oysters and their liquor to a simmer in a medium pan, adding a little water, if necessary. Poach gently for 1 or 2 minutes, or until their edges curl and they plump up. Drain the oysters, reserving the liquor. Add 1¼ cups of the liquor to the vegetables. Add the parsley, Worcestershire sauce, lemon juice, Tabasco sauce, and salt, and simmer until thickened.

Drain the artichokes, and put the oysters and artichokes in a shallow casserole. Cover them with the sauce. The recipe can be prepared ahead of time up to this point.

Preheat the oven to 350° F. In a skillet, melt the remaining 2 tablespoons butter and toss with the bread crumbs until they are well coated. Sprinkle the crumbs over the casserole. Bake for 15 to 20 minutes, or until the bread crumbs are browned and the sauce is bubbly.

SERVES 4

Almost extinct early in the century, the snowy egrets that roost in Bird City on Avery Island now number in the thousands.

JUDY McILHENNY'S CRAWFISH ÉTOUFFÉE

‖

Although crawfish have limited availability outside of the South, we would be remiss not to include at least one beloved "mudbug" recipe. Now that crawfish are farmed in Louisiana, they can be obtained partially cooked and peeled. My wife's recipe for crawfish étouffée is simple and unembellished, allowing the wonderful taste of the crawfish to come through. You can order crawfish from the mail order companies listed on page 142.

1	cup (2 sticks) butter
1½	cups chopped onion
1	cup chopped green pepper
1	cup chopped celery
3	garlic cloves, minced
1	teaspoon salt, or to taste
1	teaspoon Tabasco pepper sauce
2	tablespoons crawfish fat (see Note)
2	pounds shelled crawfish tails (about 6 to 7 pounds in the shell)
	Juice of ½ lemon
½	cup chopped fresh parsley
½	cup chopped green onions, green part only
	Cooked rice

In a Dutch oven or large heavy pot, melt the butter and cook the onion, pepper, celery, and garlic until soft, about 5 minutes. Add the salt, Tabasco sauce, and crawfish fat, and cook, uncovered, over medium-low heat for 30 minutes, stirring occasionally. Add the crawfish tails, lemon juice, and parsley. Cook for another 10 to 15 minutes. Just before serving, add the chopped green onions.

For the best flavor, prepare this dish the day before. Remove from the refrigerator an hour before serving, and reheat just until hot to avoid overcooking the crawfish. Serve over steamed white rice.

SERVES 6 TO 8

NOTE: If you cannot purchase crawfish fat separately, you can extract it from the crawfish by running the sealed package of tails under hot water to make the fat more liquid. Cut open the package and empty it into a colander with a bowl underneath to catch the fat that runs off.

CRAWFISH

The famous mudbugs of Louisiana, crawfish (des ecrevisses) are in season for about six months of the year, from December to June. The rest of the time they burrow six or more feet under the damp soil of the Louisiana wetlands. Resembling miniature lobsters, these tiny crustaceans weigh only an ounce or so, and their tails are delicious in bisque and gumbo, étouffée, and especially deep-fried (Cajun popcorn). A seasonal Louisiana tradition is whole crawfish boiled in a peppery broth along with corn, whole onions, and unpeeled potatoes, and served up in quantity with plenty of paper napkins. An experienced crawfish eater will quickly pinch the tail meat out of the shell and suck the body cavity, or "head."

FROG LEGS PIQUANT

II

TABASCO CLASSIC Nothing's more fun and mysterious than going frog hunting on a dark, hot, humid summer night in Miss Sadie's pond, a stone's throw behind my place, which we call Froggy Bottom because of its proximity to the pond. The legs of the bullfrogs on Avery Island can be big as chicken drumsticks, and are outstanding fare. We figure on two or three per person. If you can't get frog legs, simply substitute chicken or catfish.

2	tablespoons vegetable oil
¼	cup all-purpose flour
3	tablespoons butter
1	large onion, diced
1	celery stalk, diced
½	green pepper, diced
3	garlic cloves, minced
1	6-ounce can tomato paste
1	16-ounce can whole tomatoes, drained, chopped, liquid reserved
4	cups chicken broth
1	teaspoon Tabasco pepper sauce
1	teaspoon Worcestershire sauce
½	teaspoon freshly ground black pepper
15	to 20 large frog legs (about 3 pounds)
	Salt
	Cayenne pepper

In a large saucepan over medium-high heat, combine the oil and 2 tablespoons of the flour to make a roux, stirring constantly until it is light to medium brown, about 15 minutes. Stir in the butter. Add the onion, celery, green pepper, and garlic, and sauté for about 5 minutes, or until soft. Add the tomato paste, and cook over medium heat for about 10 minutes, stirring frequently. Add the tomatoes with the liquid, chicken broth, Tabasco sauce, Worcestershire sauce, and black pepper. Cover and simmer over low heat for 45 minutes.

Meanwhile, dust the frog legs with the remaining 2 tablespoons flour, seasoned with a small amount of salt and cayenne pepper. Coat a large skillet with nonstick cooking spray or a small amount of oil, add the frog legs, and sauté until lightly browned, about 3 minutes on each side. Add the legs to the sauce and simmer, covered, for an additional 15 minutes. Serve over steamed rice.

SERVES 6

NOTE: If using cut-up chicken, sauté the pieces 5 to 10 minutes longer, until nearly cooked through, and simmer in the sauce for 25 minutes. If using catfish fillets, add directly to the sauce and simmer for 20 minutes.

RED SNAPPER STEW

||

This stew, fragrant with thyme and allspice, can be made with fillets of any fine-textured white fish.

    2 garlic cloves, minced
    1 tablespoon chopped fresh parsley
    2 teaspoons salt
    1 teaspoon dried thyme
    1 bay leaf
    ½ teaspoon ground allspice
    1 tablespoon vegetable oil
   1¼ pounds red snapper or white fish fillets
    2 tablespoons butter or margarine
    1 cup chopped onion
    ¼ cup chopped green pepper
    ⅛ teaspoon powdered saffron
    2 16-ounce cans whole tomatoes, undrained, chopped
    1 teaspoon Tabasco pepper sauce
    ¾ pound fresh okra or 1 10-ounce package frozen
       okra, thawed, cut into 1-inch pieces
    ½ pound medium shrimp, shelled and deveined
       Cooked rice

In a medium bowl, mash together the garlic, parsley, 1½ teaspoons salt, thyme, bay leaf, allspice, and oil, forming a paste. Spread the mixture on the fish and set aside.

In a large pot, melt the butter over medium heat. Add the onion, pepper, and saffron, and cook for 5 minutes. Add the tomatoes and liquid, the remaining ½ teaspoon salt, and the Tabasco sauce, and simmer, uncovered, for 10 minutes. Add the fish, okra, and shrimp. Simmer the stew, uncovered, for 5 minutes, or until the fish flakes easily when pierced with a fork. Serve hot over rice.

SERVES 6

Culling the best peppers along the headland, the dirt road that separates the fields.

BROILED FISH STEAKS
WITH FRESH GINGER SAUCE

♦♦♦

A winning recipe in a catfish contest called for marinating a whole fish in an entire bottle of Tabasco pepper sauce. Although not for the faint of palate, we thought it was excellent. Somewhat more subdued, this sauce can be as hot as you like it—just add more Tabasco sauce.

- 1 cup water
- 2 teaspoons cornstarch
- 2 tablespoons sesame oil
- 3 tablespoons chopped fresh ginger
- 2 garlic cloves, minced
- 2 tablespoons soy sauce
- 2 teaspoons anchovy paste
- 1 teaspoon sugar
- 1 teaspoon Tabasco pepper sauce
- ½ cup sliced green onions
- 4 6-ounce fish steaks, such as halibut, swordfish, snapper, or tuna
- Vegetable oil
- Salt and freshly ground black pepper

Preheat the broiler. Mix together the water and cornstarch and set aside. In a medium saucepan, heat the sesame oil and sauté the ginger and garlic for 1 minute. Stir in the soy sauce, anchovy paste, sugar, and Tabasco sauce, and cook over low heat for 2 minutes, stirring constantly. Add the cornstarch, and stir constantly until the mixture comes to

Use ¼ cup olive oil plus 1 teaspoon Tabasco sauce to make a zippy "brush-on" for fish steaks.

●

a boil and thickens. Boil for 1 minute, then stir in the green onions. Set aside.

Brush the fish steaks with oil, rub them lightly with salt and pepper, and place them in an oiled broiler pan. Broil the steaks 2 to 3 inches from the heat for 5 to 7 minutes, or until they appear opaque and flake easily when probed with a fork. Remove the fish to a serving platter. Spoon 2 tablespoons of sauce over each steak, and serve the rest on the side.

SERVES 4

COURTBOUILLON

The *Petit Anse Amateur,* published by the Avery and McIllhenny children on Avery Island in 1880, offered the following recipe for courtbouillon, a fish stew generally made of redfish: "Take the head and shoulders of a fish weighing from 5 to 8 pounds, cut the solid part in thick slices and split the head in two; have ready one or two large onions very thinly sliced, half a dozen Irish potatoes sliced thinly, and one quarter of a pound best mess pork thinly sliced; black and red pepper, flour, a large tablespoonful of butter, or two of sweet oil, a tumbler of claret wine, three or four cloves, and a little allspice." Tabasco sauce was added after the stew had cooked awhile.

HOT GRILLED TROUT

||||

Charcoal-grilled fish takes on a new level of flavor when marinated in this wonderful sauce, intensified by a full tablespoon of Tabasco sauce.

- ¼ cup fresh lemon juice
- 2 tablespoons melted butter or margarine
- 2 tablespoons vegetable oil
- 2 tablespoons chopped fresh parsley
- 2 tablespoons sesame seeds
- 1 tablespoon Tabasco pepper sauce
- 1 teaspoon grated fresh ginger
- ½ teaspoon salt
- 4 whole brook trout (about 1 pound each), cleaned

For a fat-free sauce for grilled fish or chicken, puree 1 cup roasted, peeled, and seeded red pepper and add ¼ teaspoon Tabasco sauce.

Prepare a charcoal fire for grilling. In a shallow dish, mix the lemon juice, butter, oil, parsley, sesame seeds, Tabasco sauce, ginger, and salt. With a fork, pierce the skin of each fish in several places. Roll the fish in the lemon juice mixture to coat thoroughly. Leave the fish in the marinade, cover the dish, and refrigerate for 30 minutes to 1 hour, turning the fish occasionally.

Remove the fish, reserving the marinade, and place them in a hand-held hinged grill. Brush the fish with the marinade. Cook about 4 inches from the hot coals for 5 minutes. Turn, brush with marinade, and cook for 5 minutes longer, or until the flesh appears opaque and flakes easily.

SERVES 4

Salmon Steaks with Cucumber Sauce

Tabasco sauce nicely sparks this simple recipe for broiled salmon steaks, with a contrasting cool sour cream and cucumber sauce.

½   **pint sour cream**
½   **teaspoon Tabasco pepper sauce**
1   **cup diced unpeeled cucumber**
¼   **teaspoon salt**
1   **tablespoon minced fresh dill**
4   **tablespoons melted butter**
4½   **teaspoons fresh lime or lemon juice**
4   **6- to 8-ounce salmon steaks, 1 inch thick**
   Salt to taste
   Lemon slices

Blend together the sour cream and ¼ teaspoon of the Tabasco sauce in a medium bowl. Stir in the cucumber, salt, and dill. Set aside.

Preheat the broiler. In a small bowl, combine the butter, lime juice, and remaining ¼ teaspoon Tabasco sauce. Place the salmon steaks on a greased broiler rack. Sprinkle them lightly with salt and pour on the butter mixture. Broil 4 inches from the heat for 5 minutes per side, or until the flesh appears opaque. Garnish with lemon slices, and serve the sauce on the side.

Serves 4

EULA MAE'S
JAMBALAYA

‖

TABASCO CLASSIC Jambalaya is a Spanish-Creole one-pot meal made with rice and whatever is on hand—shrimp, chicken, oysters, sausage, crabs, cowpeas, or turkey. Everyone has their own version, and this is Eula Mae's. She says that scraping up all the browned bits from the bottom of the pot gives her jambalaya its special color and flavor.

1 3-pound chicken, boned and skinned, or 1½ pounds skinless, boneless breasts and thighs, cut into 1-inch cubes
1 teaspoon salt
⅛ teaspoon freshly ground black pepper
⅛ teaspoon cayenne pepper
2 tablespoons vegetable oil
½ pound cooked ham, cut into ½-inch cubes
2 large onions, chopped
1 medium green pepper, seeded and chopped
1 cup chopped celery
4 garlic cloves, peeled
3 cups chicken broth
1 16-ounce can whole tomatoes, drained and juice reserved, chopped
2 tablespoons chopped fresh parsley
½ cup chopped green onions
2 pounds medium shrimp, peeled and deveined
1 teaspoon Tabasco pepper sauce
2 cups rice, rinsed and drained

Sprinkle the chicken cubes with the salt and black and red peppers. Add the oil to a large heavy pot or Dutch oven over medium heat, and cook the chicken, stirring, until browned on all sides, about 8 to 10 minutes. Remove the chicken to a bowl. Add the ham to the pot and sauté for about 5 minutes, or until lightly browned, then add it to the chicken. Put the onions, green pepper, celery, and garlic in the pot and sauté for about 5 minutes, scraping the bottom to incorporate all the browned bits. Add the chicken and ham, reduce the heat to low, cover, and cook for 25 minutes, stirring occasionally. Add the chicken broth and reserved tomato juice to the pot, cover, and simmer for 45 minutes.

Mash the cooked garlic against the side of the pan and stir into the mixture. Add the tomatoes, parsley, green onions, shrimp, and Tabasco sauce, and adjust the seasoning to taste. Add the rice. Cover the pot, bring to a boil, lower the heat, and, stirring occasionally, simmer, covered, for 25 to 30 minutes, until the rice is tender and fluffy and the liquid is absorbed.

SERVES 6 TO 8

JAMBALAYA

Jambalaya, derived from *jambon,* the French word for ham, and *alaya,* which means rice in an African dialect, is a wonderful conglomeration of sausages, chicken, ham, and seafood cooked with rice. It is a Louisiana tradition, favored by Cajuns and Creoles alike. The rice absorbs all the flavors of the basic seasonings, which include onions, bell peppers, tomatoes, garlic, herbs, scallions, and, of course, Tabasco pepper sauce. The variations are infinite, and they're all delicious.

Pepper plant seedlings are
carefully nurtured in the
greenhouse before planting.

COUNTRY CAPTAIN CHICKEN

||

This chicken and rice dish has graced southern tables for many a generation and continues to be popular today. It was a favorite of FDR, a close friend of my great-uncle John Avery McIlhenny. Roosevelt would visit Uncle John in Virginia on his way back from Warm Springs, Georgia, and enjoy this chicken smothered in a blend of curry powder, garlic, pepper sauce, and currants.

⅓ cup all-purpose flour
½ teaspoon salt
½ teaspoon paprika
1 3-pound broiler-fryer chicken, cut up
2 tablespoons vegetable oil
1 large yellow onion, chopped
1½ large green peppers, seeded and chopped
2 large garlic cloves, minced
2 tablespoons minced fresh parsley
1 tablespoon curry powder
1 16-ounce can whole tomatoes, with juice
½ cup dried currants
1 teaspoon Tabasco pepper sauce
2 cups cooked rice
½ cup toasted slivered almonds

In a plastic bag, mix the flour, salt, and paprika. Shake the chicken pieces in the bag to coat with the flour mixture. In a large Dutch oven or heavy saucepan, heat the oil over medium-high heat and brown the chicken, turning several times. Remove the chicken to a warm platter.

In the drippings remaining in the pot over low heat, sauté the onion, peppers, garlic, parsley, and curry powder for 5 minutes, or until the vegetables are tender. Add the tomatoes and their liquid, the currants, and the Tabasco sauce, and mix well. Return the chicken to the pot, pushing it down into the sauce and ladling sauce over it. Cover and simmer over low heat for 30 minutes, or until the chicken is tender, turning the pieces occasionally. Adjust seasonings to taste. Serve the chicken on a bed of rice, and sprinkle slivered almonds on top.

SERVES 4

CHEERING UP THE MILITARY

From 1898, when Lord Kitchener took Tabasco sauce with him on his relief expedition to Khartoum in the Sudan, Tabasco sauce has been appreciated by the military. My cousin Walter Stauffer McIlhenny, who was affectionately nicknamed "Tabasco Mac," came up with the *Charley Ration Cookbook, or No Food Is Too Good for the Man Up Front* to help troops in Vietnam make their rations taste better. The recipes showed soldiers how to spice up their C-rations with Tabasco sauce to create dishes like "battlefield fufu" and "combat zone burgoo," also injecting a little humor into otherwise grim eating conditions.

Thousands of copies went to soldiers, wrapped around two-ounce bottles of Tabasco sauce in special waterproof canisters. When field rations changed, he published a new booklet using the updated "meals ready to eat" (MRE) rations, and during Desert Shield and Desert Storm Tabasco sauce miniatures were included in every third MRE packet sent to troops in the Gulf. Hundreds of them wrote to say "thanks."

In a letter dated July 31, 1991, General H. Norman Schwarzkopf wrote, "Your product has always been in demand by troops in the field. I have enjoyed spicing up my own rations with your pepper sauce for many years. During Operation Desert Shield and Desert Storm the young service men and women appreciated any touch of home and your product was certainly among the most sought after." Responding to enthusiasm like this, the military now packs Tabasco pepper sauce in *every* individual MRE pack.

CHICKEN OLÉ MOLE

II

Mexico, the birthplace of our special hot peppers, is also home to more mole sauces than one can count. This simplified version uses Tabasco sauce in place of chilies.

- 2 tablespoons olive oil
- 1 2- to 3-pound chicken, cut into pieces
- ½ cup finely chopped onion
- ½ cup finely chopped green pepper
- 1 small garlic clove, minced
- ¼ cup slivered almonds
- ¼ cup raisins
- 1½ tablespoons toasted sesame seeds
- ½ to 1 cup chicken broth
- 1 8-ounce can tomato sauce
- 1½ ounces unsweetened chocolate
- 1 teaspoon Tabasco pepper sauce
- ½ teaspoon ground cinnamon
- ¼ teaspoon ground allspice

Heat 1 tablespoon of the oil in a large skillet and brown the chicken pieces over medium heat. Remove and set aside. Add the remaining tablespoon of oil to the skillet, and sauté the onion, pepper, and garlic for 3 to 5 minutes.

In a food processor or blender, finely grind the almonds, raisins, and sesame seeds to a paste. Add the mixture to the vegetables, along with ½ cup of the broth, the tomato sauce, chocolate, Tabasco sauce, cinnamon, and allspice. Cook, stirring, until the chocolate melts.

Return the chicken to the skillet, coating the pieces well with the sauce. If the sauce is too thick, add a little more broth, about ½ cup. Cover and simmer over low heat for 30 to 40 minutes, or until the chicken is cooked through.

SERVES 4

DEVIL'S CHICKEN

llll

After Jeff Smith, better known as "The Frugal Gourmet," visited Avery Island with chef Craig Wollan, he sent us his favorite Tabasco sauce recipe, a grilled or broiled butterflied chicken said to be straight from the devil. The abundant black pepper complements the Tabasco sauce in this simple but distinctive dish.

1 3- to 4-pound chicken
½ cup olive oil
2 tablespoons Tabasco pepper sauce
   Juice of 2 lemons
1 tablespoon freshly ground black pepper, or to taste
1 teaspoon salt

Add ½ teaspoon of Tabasco sauce to the liquid used to moisten stuffing for turkey or chicken.

Using poultry shears, cut the chicken open by cutting down the backbone. Flatten it a bit by pounding with your hand so that the chicken is butterflied. Mix the remaining ingredients in a large bowl and marinate the chicken for 2 hours.

Prepare a charcoal fire for grilling or preheat the broiler. Grill the chicken, skin side down, on a medium-hot charcoal barbecue for 25 minutes, or broil it, skin side up, 5 inches below the heat for about 15 minutes. Turn and cook until the juices run clear when the thickest part is pricked with a fork, abut 15 to 20 minutes. As the chicken cooks, baste it with the marinade.

MAKES 4 SERVINGS

INDIVIDUAL SUGAR SNAP PEA & CHICKEN POT PIES

Untraditional but delicious, these shortcut chicken pot pies look spectacular with their puff pastry bonnets. They are a great way to use up leftover roast chicken.

    2½ cups chicken broth
     1 baking potato, peeled and cut into ½-inch cubes
    1½ cups sliced carrots, cut ½ inch thick
     1 cup frozen pearl onions
     ½ teaspoon dried rosemary
     ½ teaspoon Tabasco pepper sauce
     ¼ teaspoon salt
     1 red pepper, seeded and coarsely diced
     4 ounces (about 1 cup) sugar snap peas, trimmed and
        halved lengthwise
     3 tablespoons butter or margarine
     ¼ cup all-purpose flour
     8 ounces cooked chicken breast meat, cut into
        1 x 3-inch strips
     1 sheet frozen puff pastry, defrosted
     1 egg, beaten with 1 teaspoon water

In a large heavy saucepan, bring the chicken broth to a boil over high heat. Add the potato, carrots, onions, rosemary, Tabasco sauce, and salt. Reduce the heat to medium, cover, and simmer for 8 to 10 minutes, until the vegetables are tender. Add the pepper and peas and boil for 30 seconds, just until the peas turn bright green. Drain the vegetables in a colander set over a bowl to catch the chicken broth. Set aside.

Melt the butter in a saucepan over low heat. Stir in the flour and cook for 3 to 4 minutes, stirring constantly. Pour in 2 cups of the reserved chicken broth and whisk until smooth. Bring to a boil over medium heat, stirring constantly. Reduce the heat to low and simmer for 5 minutes, until thickened and bubbly, stirring frequently.

Preheat the oven to 475° F. Put the chicken strips in the bottoms of four lightly buttered ramekins or soufflé dishes. Top the chicken with the vegetables. Spoon the sauce equally into the ramekins. On a floured surface, cut the pastry into 4 rectangles. Brush the outside of the ramekin rims with some of the egg mixture. Place a pastry rectangle over each ramekin and press firmly around the edges to seal. Trim the dough to make a neat edge, and brush the tops with the egg mixture. Put the ramekins on a baking sheet and bake for 10 to 12 minutes, until the pastry is puffed and well browned. Serve at once.

SERVES 4

The making and worldwide marketing of Tabasco sauce are directed from company headquarters on Avery Island.

VENISON CHOPS
MARCHAND DE MUSCADINE

▮▮▮

TABASCO CLASSIC Avery Island and the country around it abound in game, especially wild ducks and geese, snipe, woodcock, doves, and deer. We age our venison for at least four weeks and cook it rare. We use muscadine jelly from Callaway Gardens for our sauce, but you can use any flavorful fruit jelly, such as grape or guava. If your hunter came home empty-handed, you can order venison from the sources listed on page 142.

8	4-ounce venison chops, about ½ inch thick
1¼	teaspoons Tabasco pepper sauce
	Salt
½	cup (1 stick) butter or margarine, softened
1	tablespoon vegetable oil
½	cup sliced green onions
1	cup dry red wine
½	cup muscadine jelly
¼	teaspoon salt
	Chopped fresh parsley

Season the chops with 1 teaspoon of the Tabasco sauce and sprinkle them with salt. In a large skillet, melt 1 tablespoon of the butter and the oil over medium-high heat. In two batches, cook the chops for 5 minutes, turning once, and remove to a warm serving platter.

Melt 2 tablespoons of the butter in the same skillet. Add the green onions and cook, stirring frequently, for 3 minutes, or until tender. Stir in the wine. Bring to a boil and boil rapidly to reduce to ½ cup. Stir in the jelly until it is melted. Add the remaining ¼ teaspoon Tabasco sauce and salt to taste. Remove from the heat. Stir in the remaining

5 tablespoons butter, a tablespoon at a time, until the sauce is slightly thickened. Serve over the chops. Sprinkle with parsley.

SERVES 4

RARE DUCK

My father insisted that the only way to eat wild duck breasts was rare, and his recipe was simple: "Have a slow-gaited butler walk it on a platter through a hot kitchen." For the finer-tasting wild ducks, like teal, pintail, wood duck, mallard, and ringneck, cooking them rare to medium-rare is just right. To prepare duck breasts, with a sharp boning knife cut close to the breastbone on each side of the duck and remove the breasts. Dip each breast in melted butter, and cook in a hot skillet over high heat for 3½ minutes per side. For larger ducks like the mallard, slice the cooked breasts thin across the grain, then salt and pepper them lightly and cook for 4½ minutes on each side. Cover the slices with muscadine jelly. Serve with wild rice on the side. Use the carcasses to make duck and andouille gumbo.

CRAIG CLAIBORNE'S ULTIMATE HAMBURGER

Craig Claiborne, cookbook author and former food editor of the *New York Times*, has been a great longtime friend and Tabasco sauce fan. He says Tabasco sauce is "absolutely essential" for this hamburger, which is a holdover from his bachelor days in Chicago.

    1½   pounds ground round steak
         Salt to taste
         Freshly ground black pepper to taste
    4   tablespoons butter
    1   teaspoon Worcestershire sauce
    ½   teaspoon Tabasco pepper sauce, or to taste
         Juice of ½ lemon
    ⅓   cup finely chopped fresh parsley

Divide the meat into 4 portions and shape each into a round patty. Handle the meat lightly, pressing just enough so that it holds together. Sprinkle the bottom of a very heavy skillet, preferably black iron, with a very light layer of salt, and heat the skillet until it is searingly hot. Add the patties and sear well on each side. Using a pancake turner, quickly turn the patties and reduce the heat. Cook the patties to the desired degree of doneness, 3 minutes or longer. When the hamburgers are done, sprinkle them with salt and pepper and top each with 1 tablespoon of butter. Sprinkle on the Worcestershire, Tabasco sauce, and lemon juice and transfer each hamburger to the bottom of a hamburger bun or a piece of wheat toast. Sprinkle with parsley. If a bun is used, add the top.

SERVES 4

WALTER MCILHENNY'S CHILI

||||

Walter McIlhenny was very fond of homemade chili and liked to serve his version to former Marine Corps buddies who visited him at the island.

¼ cup vegetable oil
3 pounds lean beef chuck, well trimmed, cut into
  1-inch cubes
1 cup chopped onion
3 garlic cloves, minced
3 tablespoons chili powder
2 teaspoons ground cumin
2 teaspoons salt
2 teaspoons Tabasco pepper sauce
3 cups water
1 4-ounce can chopped green chilies, drained
  Cooked rice
  Chopped onion, shredded cheese, and sour cream
  (optional)

In a 5-quart Dutch oven or heavy saucepan, heat the oil over medium-high heat. In three batches, brown the beef well, removing each batch with a slotted spoon. Set aside.

Add the onion and garlic to the pot and cook for 5 minutes, or until tender, stirring frequently. Stir in the chili powder, cumin, salt, and Tabasco sauce, and cook for 1 minute. Add the water and chilies and bring to a boil. Return the beef to the pot. Reduce the heat and simmer, uncovered, 1½ hours, or until the beef is tender. Serve the chili over rice with onion, cheese, and sour cream, if desired.

SERVES 4 TO 6

PERFECT
SEARED STEAKS

IIII

This is our favorite way to cook steaks outdoors on a charcoal grill, and it works well with hamburgers, too. Start with a good "steak fire" of white coals 3 to 4 inches below the grill. To test the fire, put the palm of your hand just above the grill. If you can keep it there only for as long as it takes to say "One thousand and one," the fire is ready.

> 4 New York strip or rib eye steaks, 2 inches thick
> 2⅔ teaspoons Tabasco pepper sauce
> Freshly cracked black pepper to taste
> Salt to taste

Place the steaks on a cutting board and, with the back of a spoon, briskly rub about ⅓ teaspoon Tabasco sauce and some pepper into both sides of each steak. Grill the steaks over a hot fire for about 5 minutes on each side for medium-rare.

To broil, preheat the broiler, place the seasoned steaks on an oiled broiler rack, and cook 6 inches from the heat for 4 to 5 minutes on each side for medium-rare. Add salt to taste.

SERVES 4

FIRING UP FAST FOOD

Make takeout terrific by sprinkling a few drops of Tabasco sauce on hamburgers, frankfurters, French fries, heroes or subs, tacos and burritos, onion rings, pizza, hot chicken, and fish sandwiches.

APRICOT-CURRY GLAZED RIBS

▮▮▮

Great grilled ribs with exceptional flavor and a dark, rich color are irresistible. These are excellent broiled, too.

2 tablespoons vegetable oil
1½ cups chopped onion
2 garlic cloves, minced
2 tablespoons curry powder
1½ cups apricot nectar
⅓ cup honey
½ cup cider vinegar
1½ teaspoons Tabasco pepper sauce
¾ teaspoon salt
4 pounds pork spareribs, baby back ribs, or beef ribs

Prepare a charcoal fire for grilling. In a medium saucepan, heat the oil over medium heat. Sauté the onion and garlic until golden. Stir in the curry powder, cook for 1 minute, and add the nectar, honey, vinegar, Tabasco sauce, and ½ teaspoon salt. Simmer for 10 minutes, stirring often.

Sprinkle the ribs with the remaining ¼ teaspoon salt. Arrange the ribs on a grill in a single layer over low heat, setting the grill rack as far from the coals as possible. For pork ribs, grill the meat for 15 minutes per side, then brush with the apricot glaze. Grill the ribs for 45 minutes longer, or until the meat is fork-tender, turning the meat often, and brushing with glaze each time. For beef ribs, grill for 5 minutes per side, then brush with glaze and continue basting and turning for 35 minutes longer, or until the ribs are brown and tender.

SERVES 4

Tabasco Sauce

What it is H

A Short History of Tabasco Sauce

...but one-my name is on it
cILHENNY

TABASCO
E. McILHENNY
NEW IBERIA
LOUISIANA
PEPPER SAUCE

Tabasco
gs. *Use*
nd don't
intensify
ish.
, such as
tatoes, and
oved by the
McIlhenny's

's—the little
amond-shaped

er's Book
s, prepared
nny Com-
mation for
eparation of the ... st delectable
shes. mailed on request.

Early promotional pamphlets and ads.

McILHENNY COMPANY
Drexel Building

kitchen *and on the table*

ASCO **is**

ESTABLISHED 1868.

Ilhenny's

E ORIGINAL
AND
LY GENUINE

BASCO.

MCILHENNY'S
Pickled Pepper Sauce

HOME
10651
TWO
STORES
COR· SIXTH & BROADWAY
208-10 SO. SPRING STREET

H. JEVNE·CO.
BROADWAY
4900

GEORGE H BUCHANAN COMPANY, PHILADELPHIA, PA.

NNY'S

ORIGINAL
NUINE

Tabasco

SAUCE

Mc Ilhenny's
abasco Sauce
Recipes

Prepared by
s. Sarah Tyson Rorer

GINGERED PORK ROAST

❚❚

Cajuns love roast pork. A favorite way to cook it is in a "Cajun microwave," a large wooden box with a metal pan as a cover. The recipe calls for a 100-pound pig, 20 pounds of charcoal, and a case of beer. The pig goes in the box, the charcoal is heaped on top in the pan, and the beer goes into the cook.

An easier and quite delicious version is this pork roast, infused with ginger, garlic, sage, and Tabasco sauce, often the centerpiece of holiday meals in our home. The pureed vegetables make a light and flavorful gravy.

> 1 tablespoon minced fresh ginger
> 2 garlic cloves, minced
> 1 teaspoon dried sage
> ½ teaspoon salt
> 1 5-pound loin of pork
> ⅓ cup apple jelly
> 1¼ teaspoons Tabasco pepper sauce
> 2 medium carrots, peeled and cut into ½-inch slices
> 2 medium onions, peeled and cut into ½-inch slices
> 1¾ cups water

Preheat the oven to 325° F. Mix the ginger, garlic, sage, and salt in a small dish and rub the mixture over the pork. Place the meat in a shallow roasting pan and roast for 1½ hours. Remove from the oven, then score the meat in a diamond pattern.

In a small bowl, mix the jelly and Tabasco sauce, and spread it generously over the roast. Arrange the carrots and onions around the meat, then add 1 cup of water. Roast up to 1 hour longer, or until a meat thermometer registers 170° F. Remove the roast to a serving platter and keep warm.

Skim the fat from the pan drippings, then puree the cooked vegetables and pan liquids in a food processor or blender. Stir in the remaining ¾ cup water. Reheat the gravy and serve with the roast.

SERVES 6 TO 8

CREOLE-CAJUN

The Creoles of south Louisiana are generally considered the white descendants of the French and Spanish settlers of the colonial period, most of whom lived in New Orleans and along the Mississippi River. The Cajuns, or more formally the Acadians of Louisiana, are descendants of the six thousand French who were expelled by the English from the province of Acadie in Nova Scotia in 1755; many settled in the bayou country of southwestern Louisiana around 1765. The Creoles aspire to fine city cuisine with many flavor combinations and subtle sauces. The Cajuns tend to serve real country food, such as delicious, peppery one-pot dishes.

LAMB SHANKS IN RED WINE

‖

The legendary James Beard featured lamb shanks in red wine in "Gourmet Adventures for Men on the Move," a booklet he wrote for Tabasco sauce many years ago. Here's an updated version of his recipe adding crushed tomatoes, onion, and orange zest to the wine, guaranteed to please any man—or woman—in motion.

2 tablespoons olive oil
4 lamb shanks
3 cups finely chopped onion
2 teaspoons minced garlic
2 cups dry red wine
2 cups canned crushed tomatoes
2 tablespoons chopped fresh parsley
1 strip orange zest, about 3 inches x ½ inch
1 teaspoon crumbled dried rosemary
1 bay leaf
1 teaspoon Tabasco pepper sauce
1 teaspoon sugar
½ teaspoon salt
   Freshly ground black pepper to taste
   Chopped fresh parsley for garnish

Preheat the oven to 350° F. Heat the oil in a medium Dutch oven or heavy saucepan and brown the lamb shanks in batches over medium heat. Remove the lamb and set aside.

In the same pan, sauté the onion over medium heat until tender and golden, about 5 minutes. Add the garlic and cook for 1 minute. Add the wine, turn up the heat, and boil for 2 minutes. Add the remaining ingredients, including the lamb shanks, and bring to a boil. Cover and bake for 2 hours, or until the lamb is tender, turning several times.

Discard the bay leaf and orange zest. Remove the shanks with a slotted spoon and keep warm. Cook the remaining sauce over high heat for about 5 minutes, or until slightly thickened. Pour the sauce over the shanks and serve sprinkled with parsley.

SERVES 4

A MUST FOR MEAT

A splash of Tabasco sauce is just the ticket for beef, veal, pork, lamb, and venison dishes. Brush it on the outsides of roasts, steaks, and chops; mix into burgers, meat loaf, meatballs, stew, stir-frys, stroganoff, chili, hash, and casseroles; splash it into marinades and barbecue sauces. Figure on ¼ teaspoon per pound of meat.

PEPPER-STUFFED LAMB
WITH GARLIC CHÈVRE SAUCE

This is exceptional dinner party fare, impressive-looking and superb-tasting, flavored with herbs, sun-dried tomatoes, Tabasco sauce, garlic, and chèvre.

- 2 red or green bell peppers
- 1 6- to 7-pound leg of lamb, boned and butterflied
  Salt and freshly ground black pepper to taste
- ¾ cup sun-dried tomatoes in oil, drained (about 4½ ounces)
- ¾ cup olive oil
- 2 tablespoons minced fresh rosemary leaves
- 2 tablespoons minced fresh thyme leaves
- 3 garlic cloves, minced
- 1 teaspoon Tabasco pepper sauce

GARLIC CHÈVRE SAUCE
- 1 4-ounce package chèvre (goat cheese)
- 3 garlic cloves, minced
- ½ cup light cream or half-and-half
- ¼ teaspoon Tabasco pepper sauce
- 1 rosemary sprig

Roast the peppers (see page 15).

Place the lamb skin side down on a cutting board or other surface and pat it dry. Sprinkle the meat with salt and pepper. Arrange the tomatoes and roasted peppers down the center of the lamb, then roll up the lamb, secure it with twine, and set it in a roasting pan. In a bowl, whisk the oil, herbs, garlic, and Tabasco sauce. Pour the mixture over the lamb, turning to coat. Cover and refrigerate for 24 hours, turning once or twice.

Preheat the oven to 450° F. Place the uncovered roast

in the oven and immediately reduce the heat to 325° F. Cook the lamb for 20 minutes per pound, about 2 hours, or until a meat thermometer registers 125° F. for rare or 140°F. for medium. Let the lamb stand for 15 minutes before slicing. Meanwhile, in a small saucepan over low heat, whisk together the chèvre, garlic, cream, and Tabasco sauce until the mixture is well blended and heated thoroughly. Garnish with rosemary and serve with the lamb.

SERVES 8

FINE-TUNING A PALATE

In the mid-1800s New Orleans was a prosperous Mediterranean-like city that happened to grow up on the banks of the Mississippi River. It was a crazy, fun metropolis filled with high-spirited Creoles of Spanish-French descent, and hard-charging newcomers known as "the Americans." Its restaurants and cuisine were as fine as any on the Continent. And it was here that Edmund McIlhenny became a true gourmet, developing his love of fine food, especially condiments, sauces, and spices.

MUSTARD CRUSTED LEG OF LAMB

With a name like McIlhenny you know we like lamb. This well-coated leg is good either hot or at room temperature. If there's any left, it makes superb sandwiches.

2 tablespoons olive oil
½ cup Dijon-style mustard
2 tablespoons soy sauce
1 garlic clove, minced
¼ teaspoon ground ginger
½ teaspoon Tabasco pepper sauce
1 teaspoon dried thyme
1 tablespoon chopped fresh chives
1 6-pound leg of lamb
½ cup fine dry bread crumbs

In medium bowl, combine the oil, mustard, soy sauce, garlic, ginger, Tabasco sauce, thyme, and chives. Place the lamb on a rack in a roasting pan. Coat the lamb with the mustard mixture, sprinkle it with the bread crumbs, and let it stand for 1 hour.

Preheat the oven to 350° F. Roast the lamb for 1½ hours, or until a meat thermometer registers 130° F. for medium-rare or 145°F. for medium.

SERVES 8

VEGETABLES & SIDE DISHES

MELLOW CABBAGE SALAD

This cabbage slaw, enriched with mustard, herbs, and honey, is excellent served alongside meat, poultry, or fish.

½ teaspoon salt
Freshly ground black pepper to taste
1 tablespoon cider vinegar
1 tablespoon beef broth (optional)
2 tablespoons Dijon mustard
1 tablespoon honey
½ teaspoon Tabasco pepper sauce
¼ cup olive oil
4 cups finely shredded cabbage
3 tablespoons chopped green onions
2 tablespoons chopped fresh dill
1 teaspoon celery seed

In a large bowl, whisk together the salt, pepper, vinegar, broth, mustard, honey, and Tabasco sauce. Slowly whisk in the oil. Add the remaining ingredients and toss well to blend. Cover and chill. Serve with additional Tabasco sauce, if desired.

SERVES 4 TO 6

SUMATRA SALAD

This simple but rather exotic composed salad marries crisp fresh vegetables and smooth tofu with a spicy peanut dressing for an unusual Indonesian-inspired taste.

SALAD
1 pound fresh green beans, trimmed
2 cups shredded cabbage
2 large carrots, cut into julienne
1 cucumber, cut diagonally into ¼-inch slices
1 cup bean sprouts
8 ounces tofu, cut into ½-inch cubes

DRESSING
⅓ cup smooth peanut butter
⅓ cup water
2 tablespoons fresh lemon juice
1¼ teaspoons Tabasco pepper sauce
½ teaspoon salt
1 garlic clove, cut in half
1 piece lemon zest, about 1 inch
¼ cup vanilla yogurt

One-quarter teaspoon of Tabasco sauce perks up any salad dressing. Use more for a spicier taste.

Steam the beans, cabbage, and carrots 2 to 3 minutes, or until tender-crisp, and cool. Arrange the cooked vegetables, cucumber, sprouts, and tofu on a serving platter.

In a small saucepan, mix the peanut butter, water, lemon juice, Tabasco sauce, salt, garlic, and lemon peel, and stir over low heat until smooth. Remove from the heat and discard the garlic and lemon zest. Stir in the yogurt. Serve the dressing warm over the salad.

SERVES 4 TO 6

SPIRITED SQUASH

Onion, thyme, and Tabasco sauce liven up butternut squash in this simple but very good recipe.

- 1 **butternut squash (about 1¾ pounds), peeled and seeded**
- ¼ **cup water**
- ¼ **cup chopped onion**
- ½ **teaspoon dried thyme**
- 1 **tablespoon butter or margarine**
- ¼ **teaspoon salt**
- ½ **teaspoon Tabasco pepper sauce**

Cut the squash into 1-inch cubes. In a medium saucepan, combine the squash, water, onion, and thyme. Cover the pan tightly and cook over low heat for 20 to 25 minutes, or until the squash is tender. Mash the squash with the remaining ingredients.

SERVES 4

NOTE: To microwave, combine the squash, 2 tablespoons water, and the onion and thyme in a medium-size microwave-safe dish. Cover and cook on high for 8 to 10 minutes, until the squash is tender. Mash the squash. Stir in the butter, salt, and Tabasco sauce.

TABASCO SAUCE
CAPTURES THE WORLD

Tabasco sauce is labeled in fifteen languages for shipment to more than a hundred countries.

After the United States, Japan consumes more Tabasco sauce than any other country. The Japanese splash it on pizza and spaghetti. In Belgium it is always included in "filet américain," the Belgian name for steak tartare. In Israel, where it was introduced about thirty years ago by sailors and diplomats, it is used most frequently on the ubiquitous falafel. Oil workers brought it to the United Arab Emirates, where it is popular in dishes like tabouleh and sambossa.

In Italy hot pepper seasoning has been adopted by southern Italians as an alternative to expensive Eastern spices. They find it a good combination with olive oil, the "elixir of strength and life." In France Tabasco sauce is considered a trendy product, found mostly in urban centers like Paris, and used in tomato juice and steak tartare. In Canada the favorite use is in the Bloody Caesar, a tomato and clam juice drink concocted in Calgary in the 1970s. Australians put it in potent drinks with names like Rambo, Rocky, and Dirty Harry.

Tabasco is riding the tide of change in Sweden and the Netherlands, where the basic, mellower seasonings such as salt and pepper, cinnamon, ginger, allspice, and bay leaf are giving ways to hotter, spicier tastes. In Greece it is now popular as a flavor enhancer with working women who have less time to prepare long-cooked meals. In areas where hot foods are the norm, such as Hong Kong, Thailand, and Korea, Tabasco sauce is well accepted, as it is in the cuisines of Latin America and tropical island nations around the world.

CHEESE SCONES

Hot from the oven, these scones are really good eating, especially with vegetable soup. To vary the flavor, throw in a half cup of chopped reconstituted sun-dried tomatoes, make them with cheddar cheese instead of Parmesan, or try other herbs such as basil or dill.

2 cups all-purpose flour
¾ cup grated Parmesan cheese
2 teaspoons baking powder
1 teaspoon dried oregano, crumbled
¼ teaspoon salt
4 tablespoons butter, chilled and cut into pieces
½ cup milk
2 large eggs, lightly beaten
1 teaspoon Tabasco pepper sauce
¾ cup finely chopped onion

Preheat the oven to 400° F. In a large bowl or a food processor, mix the flour, cheese, baking powder, oregano, and salt. Cut in the butter, using a pastry blender, two knives, or pulses of the food processor, until the mixture resembles coarse crumbs. Transfer the mixture to a large bowl, if blended in a food processor.

In a small bowl, stir together the milk, eggs, and Tabasco sauce. Make a well in the center of the dry ingredients and add the milk mixture, stirring to combine. Mix in the onion. The dough will be sticky.

Lightly butter a baking sheet. With lightly floured hands, pat the dough into a 9-inch circle in the center of the baking sheet. Cut the circle into 8 wedges. Bake the scones for 20 to 25 minutes, or until lightly browned.

MAKES 8

Early on, the final straining of the sauce was done by hand, then called "pounding," as the sauce was pounded through a fine mesh screen.

LOUISIANA YAM MUFFINS

Coffee, cinnamon, and Tabasco pepper sauce give these yam muffins a marvelous and unusual flavor. When you're mashing up yams or sweet potatoes for dinner, remember to save some to make these easy muffins the next day. If you wish, add a half cup of chopped pecans to the batter.

- 1 cup all-purpose flour
- 1 cup stone-ground yellow cornmeal
- ¼ cup sugar
- 1 tablespoon baking powder
- 1¼ teaspoons ground cinnamon
- ½ teaspoon salt
- 2 large eggs, lightly beaten
- ½ cup cold strong coffee
- 4 tablespoons melted butter or margarine
- 1 cup mashed yams or sweet potatoes
- ½ teaspoon Tabasco pepper sauce

Preheat the oven to 425° F. Grease twelve 3 x 1½-inch muffin cups. In a large bowl, mix together the flour, cornmeal, sugar, baking powder, cinnamon, and salt. In a medium bowl, stir together the eggs, coffee, butter, yams, and Tabasco sauce. Make a well in the center of the dry ingredients. Add the yam mixture and stir just to combine. Spoon the batter into the muffin cups. Bake for 20 to 25 minutes, or until a cake tester inserted in the center comes out clean. Cool for 5 minutes on a wire rack, then remove the muffins from the pans. Serve warm or at room temperature.

MAKES 12

Note: To microwave the muffins, spoon about ⅓ cup of batter into each of 6 paper baking cup–lined 6-ounce custard cups or microwave-safe muffin pan cups. Giving the cups or muffin pan half a turn once during cooking, cook, uncovered, on high for 4 to 5½ minutes, until a cake tester inserted in the center comes out clean. Cool for 5 minutes on a wire rack, then remove from the pans. Repeat with the remaining batter.

LUNCHTIME LIFTERS

A miniature bottle of Tabasco sauce (available from Avery Island) is a cheerful addition to a lunch box, or tucked into a pocket for traveling. Sprinkle a drop or two of Tabasco sauce on meat and cheese sandwiches. Add it to chicken, tuna, egg, or potato salad, cole slaw, and deviled eggs. Use a few drops to enliven the mayonnaise or dressing used for sandwiches.

PIQUANT ONIONS

No holiday meal is complete without these onions. They are a perfect flavor foil for turkey, ham, duck, roast beef, or roast pork. It's a hassle to peel the little onions, but well worth it.

- 2 pounds small white onions, peeled
- 2 tablespoons butter or margarine
- 1 13¾-ounce can beef broth (not condensed)
- 1 8-ounce can tomato sauce
- 3 tablespoons cider vinegar
- ⅔ cup seedless dark raisins
- 1 tablespoon sugar
- ¼ teaspoon crumbled dried thyme
- 1 bay leaf
- 1 tablespoon water
- 1 tablespoon cornstarch
- ½ teaspoon Tabasco pepper sauce

Cut an **X** in the stem ends of the onions to prevent them from splitting. In a 10-inch skillet over medium heat, melt the butter and lightly brown the onions. Add the broth, tomato sauce, vinegar, raisins, sugar, thyme, and bay leaf. Cover and bring to a boil, then reduce the heat and simmer for 40 to 45 minutes, or until the onions are tender. Remove the bay leaf.

In a small cup, combine the water and cornstarch. Stir into the onions and add the Tabasco sauce. Cook, stirring, for 1 or 2 minutes, until the mixture boils and thickens.

SERVES 6 TO 8

A BARRAGE OF BILLBOARDS

In 1890, the year of Grandpère's death, my great-uncle John Avery McIlhenny took over the modest Tabasco sauce business. He toured the country, meeting the storeowners and promoting Tabasco sauce with a barrage of billboards, demonstrations, giveaways, contests, and even a burlesque opera called *Tabasco,* first staged by Harvard's Hasty Pudding Club. A veteran of the Rough Riders' siege of San Juan Hill in Cuba, Uncle John left the company in 1906 to accept an appointment to the U.S. Civil Service Commission at the behest of his good friend Teddy Roosevelt.

Above: A Tabasco bottle–shaped guitar is the pride of this Zydeco musician.
Right: Ned Simmons, the president of McIlhenny Company, is greeted in appropriate fashion by the pelican mascot at the opening of the New Orleans World Expo in 1984.Far right: Scarlet Yerger, Miss Louisiana Teenager 1982, wears a Tabasco bottle costume.

HONEY-GLAZED CARROTS

||

Carrots are far from common when teamed with golden raisins, honey, lemon, ginger, and almonds. Tabasco pepper sauce effectively balances the sweet taste.

    1   pound carrots, peeled and thinly sliced
    ¼   cup golden raisins
    2   tablespoons butter or margarine
    3   tablespoons honey
    1   tablespoon fresh lemon juice
    ¼   teaspoon ground ginger
    ¼   teaspoon Tabasco pepper sauce
    ¼   cup sliced unpeeled almonds (optional)

Preheat oven to 375° F.

In a medium saucepan cook the carrots in ½ inch of boiling water, covered, over medium heat for 8 minutes. Drain the carrots, then turn into a 1-quart baking dish. Stir in the raisins, butter, honey, lemon juice, ginger, and Tabasco sauce. Bake, uncovered, for 25 to 30 minutes; stir occasionally until the carrots are glazed. Spoon into a serving bowl. Sprinkle with almonds, if desired.

SERVES 4

NOTE: To microwave the carrots, combine the butter, honey, lemon juice, ginger, and Tabasco pepper sauce in a 1½-quart microwave-safe casserole. Microwave on high 45 seconds until the butter is melted. Stir to blend. Stir in the carrots. Cover and microwave on high 8 to 10 minutes, stirring after 4 minutes. Remove from the oven. Sprinkle with almonds, if desired.

OKRA CREOLE STYLE

The tapered green pods called okra, or févi, came to Louisiana from Africa. In this dish, the okra's rich, earthy flavor is enhanced by the traditional Creole vegetables and a splash of Tabasco sauce. For best results, simmer it slowly until tender.

1 tablespoon butter
1 onion, minced
1 garlic clove, minced
1 green pepper, finely chopped
3 tomatoes, peeled, seeded, and chopped, juice reserved
1 teaspoon chopped fresh parsley
½ teaspoon Tabasco pepper sauce
¾ teaspoon salt
 Freshly ground pepper to taste
1½ pounds (about 4 dozen) fresh okra, washed, trimmed

Melt the butter in a large enamel-lined or coated saucepan, then add the onion, garlic, and green pepper and sauté over medium heat for 4 to 5 minutes or until tender. Add the tomatoes and their juice, parsley, Tabasco sauce, and salt and pepper. Add the okra, cover, and simmer over low heat for 45 minutes, or until the okra is tender.

SERVES 6

OKRA

Okra, a vegetable long prized in Africa, was originally called *gombo* or *gumbo,* a word that has come to mean the okra-thickened soup. In Louisiana, fresh, young, tender okra with its delicious earthy flavor is served up fried, boiled, braised, in soups, stews, and innumerable other Cajun and Creole dishes.

CORN MAQUE CHOUX

A Cajun classic, Corn Maque Choux is a good example of a simple vegetable stepped up in flavor with traditional Cajun ingredients: onion, green pepper, tomato, and Tabasco pepper sauce.

    1   tablespoon butter or margarine
    ½   cup chopped onion
    ½   cup chopped green pepper
    4   cups whole-kernel corn (canned, fresh, or frozen,
        thawed)
    1   tomato, cored, seeded, and chopped
    ¼   teaspoon salt
    ½   teaspoon Tabasco pepper sauce

In a 2-quart saucepan, melt the butter over medium heat. Add the onion and pepper and, stirring frequently, cook for 5 minutes, or until tender. Stir in the corn, tomato, salt, and Tabasco sauce. Reduce the heat and simmer for 10 to 15 minutes, or until the corn is tender.

SERVES 4 TO 6

SPANISH POTATO SALAD

An unusual combination of potatoes, oranges, and red onion tossed with a piquant sauce sets this potato salad apart from the masses.

- 1 pound new potatoes, scrubbed
- 3 cups salad greens torn into small pieces
- ¼ cup sliced celery
- 1 medium red onion, thinly sliced
- 2 oranges, peeled and sectioned
- ¼ cup mayonnaise
- ¼ cup plain yogurt
- 2 tablespoons orange juice
- ½ teaspoon Tabasco pepper sauce
- ½ teaspoon salt

Pile your favorite toppings on a baked potato, like cheese, broccoli, and sour cream, then top it all off with a few drops of Tabasco sauce.

Fill a medium saucepan with ½ inch of salted water and bring to a boil. Add the potatoes, cover, and cook until done, about thirty minutes. Drain, cool, and cut into ¼-inch slices.

Line a salad bowl with the greens. On the greens, layer the potatoes, celery, onion, and orange sections. Chill.

For the dressing, beat together the mayonnaise, yogurt, orange juice, Tabasco sauce, and salt in a small bowl. Just before serving, toss the salad with the dressing.

SERVES 4

CARROT PARSNIP PURÉE

The splash of bourbon along with the Tabasco sauce balances the sweetness of the parsnips to give this dish a wonderfully mellow flavor.

- 1 pound carrots, peeled and cut into ¾-inch pieces
- 1 pound parsnips, peeled and cut into ¾-inch pieces
  Salt to taste
- 2 tablespoons heavy cream
- 2 tablespoons butter or margarine
- 1 tablespoon bourbon
- ½ teaspoon Tabasco pepper sauce
  Freshly grated nutmeg to taste
  Freshly ground black pepper to taste

In a 2-quart saucepan, cover the carrots and parsnips with cold water. Add salt and bring to a boil over medium-high heat. Reduce the heat to low, cover, and simmer for 20 to 25 minutes, or until the vegetables are tender but not mushy, then drain. Puree the vegetables with the remaining ingredients in a food processor.

SERVES 8

HERB BROILED TOMATOES

||

Quick and colorful, these are an attractive accompaniment to meat, chicken, or fish.

> 4 tomatoes
> ½ teaspoon salt
> ½ teaspoon sugar
> ½ teaspoon Tabasco pepper sauce
> 1 tablespoon melted butter or margarine
> ¼ cup fine dry bread crumbs
> ¼ teaspoon dried basil
> ¼ teaspoon dried thyme
> Chopped fresh parsley

Preheat the broiler. Cut the tops off the tomatoes. Place them cut side up on a broiler pan, and sprinkle with salt and sugar.

In a small bowl, blend the Tabasco sauce with the butter, then add the bread crumbs, basil, and thyme. Spoon the mixture over the tomatoes. Broil 3 inches from the heat for about 5 minutes. Serve sprinkled with parsley.

SERVES 4

LEMON SESAME ASPARAGUS

This simple butter sauce brings out the best in fresh asparagus. The sesame seeds add crunch and the Tabasco sauce and lemon contribute a little bite.

    2 pounds fresh asparagus
    2 teaspoons sesame seeds
    1 tablespoon butter or margarine
    2 tablespoons fresh lemon juice
    ¼ teaspoon salt
    ¼ teaspoon Tabasco pepper sauce
       Lemon slices

Wash the asparagus and break off the ends by gently bending each stalk. Steam the asparagus over boiling water for 5 to 10 minutes, just until tender-crisp. Remove to a heated serving dish and keep warm. Meanwhile, in a small skillet, brown the sesame seeds in butter, then add the lemon juice, salt, and Tabasco sauce. Pour the sauce over the asparagus, and garnish with lemon slices.

SERVES 4

ZYDECO GREEN BEANS

||||

Zydeco Green Beans is actually a redundancy. The exuberant music of Louisiana's black French-speaking Creoles is called zydeco, an idiomatic phonetic version of *les haricots*, French for snap beans. Serve these green beans as a relish, or as "stirrers" for Bloody Marys.

2¼	cups water
¾	cup white vinegar
2	tablespoons sugar
1	tablespoon mustard seeds, crushed
4	medium garlic cloves, thinly sliced
3	bay leaves
1½	teaspoons salt
1½	teaspoon Tabasco pepper sauce
1	pound green beans, trimmed

In a large saucepan, stir together the water, vinegar, sugar, mustard seeds, garlic, bay leaves, salt, and Tabasco sauce. Bring to a boil, reduce the heat, cover, and simmer for 5 minutes. Add the beans. Cover and simmer for 10 minutes, until tender-crisp. Arrange the beans in a shallow dish and cover them completely with the vinegar mixture. Cover and refrigerate overnight. Serve cold.

MAKES 1 QUART

TRAPPER'S CAMP BEANS

Even Louisiana has its cold days, when we look forward to a dish that warms the insides. This cassoulet-like dish is an authoritative one-pot meal that includes leeks and carrots along with sausage. Adding more Tabasco sauce at the table really gives it zing.

1	pound dried beans (great Northern, yellow eye, or pinto)
4½	cups cold water
¼	pound unsliced bacon or salt pork
2	leeks, cleaned and thinly sliced
2	cups chopped onion
1	onion, peeled
6	whole cloves
1	13¾-ounce can chicken broth
5	carrots, cut into 1-inch slices
3	garlic cloves, minced
2	teaspoons Tabasco pepper sauce
1	teaspoon dried thyme
1	teaspoon dried marjoram
1	teaspoon dried sage
2	bay leaves
6	whole black peppercorns
1	16-ounce can whole tomatoes, crushed
1	pound Polish sausage, cut into ½-inch slices

Rinse and pick over the beans. In a 6-quart Dutch oven or heavy ovenproof pot, soak the beans in the water overnight. Do *not* drain the beans.

In a skillet over medium heat, brown the bacon or salt pork on both sides. Remove the meat and drain on paper towels. Add the leeks and chopped onion to the skillet and cook for 10 minutes, or until tender. Add the bacon or salt pork, leeks, and chopped onion to the beans.

Stud the whole onion with cloves. Add the onion, broth, carrots, garlic, Tabasco sauce, thyme, marjoram, sage, bay leaves, and peppercorns to the beans. Bring to a boil, reduce the heat, and simmer, covered, for 1 hour, stirring occasionally. Stir in the tomatoes and sausage. Preheat the oven to 350° F. and bake the casserole, uncovered, for 1 hour, or until almost all the liquid is absorbed.

SERVES 6 TO 8

BEANS

Beans—red, white, string, or lima—have always been a mainstay in Louisiana, and become particularly flavorful with the addition of pepper sauce. Red beans and rice are a typical Monday dish, the beans simmered with the Sunday hambone, served over rice, and topped with a sprinkling of scallions. Red beans are also cooked with red wine and sausage, pork, or ham, or pureed with butter, milk, and cream to the consistency of mashed potatoes. White beans, cooked in a similar fashion, are popular with Creoles for their more delicate flavor and texture. Add a generous dash of Tabasco sauce to any bean dish, and offer additional Tabasco sauce at the table, as the heat from the sauce evaporates during long cooking.

DIRTY RICE

▌▌▌

TABASCO CLASSIC An original soul food, dirty rice is cooked white rice mixed up with chopped chicken giblets and well-seasoned vegetables. It makes a great poultry stuffing.

- ½ **pound chicken gizzards**
- ½ **pound chicken livers**
- 2 **tablespoons olive oil**
- ½ **cup chopped onion**
- ⅓ **cup chopped celery**
- ⅓ **cup chopped green pepper**
- 2 **garlic cloves, minced**
- 1½ **teaspoons salt, divided**
- ½ **teaspoon freshly ground black pepper**
- 1½ **teaspoons Tabasco pepper sauce**
- 2 **cups water**
- 1 **tablespoon butter or margarine**
- 1 **cup uncooked rice**
- ½ **cup chopped green onions**

To chop the gizzards and livers, freeze them for at least ½ hour so they are easier to handle, then chop them finely. In a large skillet heat the oil over medium heat, then add the gizzards and sauté for 5 minutes. Add the onion, celery, green pepper, garlic, ½ teaspoon salt, and pepper, and cook for 10 minutes, stirring occasionally. Add the livers and Tabasco sauce and cook over low heat for 20 minutes longer, stirring occasionally.

Meanwhile, in a medium saucepan combine the water, butter, and remaining 1 teaspoon salt. Bring the mixture to a boil and stir in the rice. Cover, then reduce the heat and simmer for 20 minutes, or until the liquid is absorbed and the rice is done. Combine the rice and giblet mixture, and stir in the chopped green onions. Serve hot.

SERVES 6 TO 8

THE TABASCO COOKBOOK

Red Beans and Rice on Monday

♦♦♦

In New Orleans, Red Beans and Rice has evolved into a traditional Monday dish, but it's a fine accompaniment anytime for fried chicken, pork chops, ham, or sausage.

1	pound dried red beans, picked over
8	cups cold water
½	pound lean salt pork, bacon, or ham, diced
1	tablespoon olive oil
1	cup chopped onion
1	garlic clove, peeled and minced
2	tablespoons chopped fresh parsley
¾	teaspoon salt
1½	teaspoons Tabasco pepper sauce
4	cups hot cooked rice

In a large saucepan combine the dried beans and the water, cover, and soak overnight. Add the pork, bacon, or ham and bring to a simmer. Cook, covered, for 15 minutes.

Meanwhile, in a medium skillet heat the oil and sauté the onion and garlic for 3 minutes or until golden. Add the mixture to the beans along with the parsley, salt, and Tabasco sauce. Cover and simmer 1½ to 1¾ hours longer, or until the beans are tender enough to mash one easily with a fork. Add hot water as needed to keep the beans covered, and stir occasionally. When the beans are finished they will have soaked up most of the liquid. Serve over the hot cooked rice.

SERVES 8

PEPPERY POLENTA
WITH TANGY TOMATO SAUCE

▮▮▮

This is our version of Italian polenta, punched up with Tabasco pepper sauce and served with a fresh tomato herb sauce. It's fabulous as a main dish or served on the side with meat or chicken.

POLENTA

4	tablespoons butter or margarine
½	cup chopped onion
4¼	cups water
1⅓	cups cornmeal
½	teaspoon salt
¾	teaspoon Tabasco pepper sauce

TANGY TOMATO SAUCE

¼	cup extra-virgin olive oil
1	cup coarsely chopped onion
2	cloves garlic, minced
3	pounds ripe tomatoes, peeled, seeded, and chopped
2	tablespoons chopped fresh basil leaves or 1 tablespoon dried basil
1	teaspoon dried oregano
1	teaspoon Tabasco pepper sauce
½	teaspoon salt

Freshly grated Parmesan cheese (optional)

Preheat the oven to 375° F. In a medium saucepan, melt 2 tablespoons of the butter and sauté the onion until golden. Stir in the water and bring to a boil. Gradually add the cornmeal, stirring constantly. Add the salt and Tabasco sauce. Stir the polenta over low heat until the mixture is very thick.

Melt the remaining 2 tablespoons butter. Brush a 1½-quart shallow round baking dish with half of it. Turn the polenta into the dish and brush the remaining butter on top. Bake for 30 to 40 minutes, or until lightly browned.

Meanwhile, in a large heavy skillet heat the oil and sauté the onion and garlic for 5 minutes, or until tender. Add the tomatoes, basil, oregano, Tabasco sauce, and salt. Bring to a boil, lower the heat, and simmer for 20 minutes. To serve, cut the polenta into wedges and sprinkle with Parmesan cheese, if desired. Serve with the sauce.

SERVES 6 TO 8

GREAT GRAINS

Grains are nutritious and comforting, but lack mouth-filling flavor on their own. Just ¼ teaspoon of Tabasco sauce per cup added to the cooking liquid really heightens their taste. Try it with bulgur, couscous, noodles, orzo, polenta, and white, brown, or wild rice dishes such as risotto and pilaf.

GARLIC-ROASTED POTATOES

||

These roasted potatoes, generously flavored with garlic, olive oil, and Tabasco sauce, stand up well to steaks, chops, burgers, or broiled chicken. Since they are cut into chunks, they take only half an hour in the oven, but are nicely crisp on the outside.

> 4   russet potatoes, unpeeled, cut into 1-inch chunks
> 2   large garlic cloves, peeled and thinly sliced
> 2   tablespoons olive oil
> 1   teaspoon Tabasco pepper sauce
> ¾   teaspoon salt

Preheat the oven to 400° F. In a large roasting pan, toss the potatoes with the remaining ingredients. Stirring once halfway through, roast the potatoes in the center of the oven for 30 minutes, or until they are tender when pierced with a fork.

SERVES 4 TO 6

CONDIMENTS & SAUCES

CHUNKY SALSA

||||

Salsa is a staple in our house. We make our own so we can have it as spicy as we like.

> 2 tablespoons olive oil
> 1 cup coarsely chopped onion
> 1 cup coarsely diced green pepper
> 1 28-ounce can tomatoes, drained and coarsely chopped, ½ cup juice reserved
> 1 tablespoon fresh lime juice
> 2 teaspoons Tabasco pepper sauce
> ½ teaspoon salt
> 2 tablespoons chopped fresh cilantro or Italian parsley

In a large heavy saucepan, heat the oil over high heat. Add the onion and pepper and sauté for 5 to 6 minutes, until tender, stirring frequently. Add the tomatoes and juice, stir, and bring to a boil. Reduce the heat to low and simmer for 6 to 8 minutes, until the salsa is slightly thickened, stirring occasionally. Remove from the heat. Stir in the lime juice, Tabasco sauce, and salt. Cool to lukewarm, then stir in the cilantro. Spoon the salsa into clean jars and seal. The salsa keeps in the refrigerator for up to 5 days.

MAKES 3 ½ CUPS

PICKLED SHALLOTS

We keep a container of these in the refrigerator to serve as a relish with cold cuts, steak, hamburgers, chicken, and a variety of other meat dishes.

- 3 pounds small shallots or pearl onions
- 2 cups white vinegar
- 2 cups water
- 6 tablespoons sugar
- 2 teaspoons crumbled dried rosemary
- 2 teaspoons salt
- 1 teaspoon Tabasco pepper sauce

Drop the shallots into a large pot of boiling water and cook for 1 minute. Drain and rinse with cold water. Cut off the roots, slip off the skins, and set aside.

In a large saucepan, combine the remaining ingredients and simmer for 3 minutes. Add the shallots and simmer for 15 minutes, until tender-crisp. Cool them slightly, then cover and refrigerate. Allow the shallots to stand for 2 to 3 days to blend flavors. They may be kept refrigerated in sealed containers for several weeks. Serve the shallots at room temperature.

MAKES 6 CUPS

BANKING ON PEPPER SEEDS

Although it seems simple, the process of growing peppers and making Tabasco pepper sauce is as much an art as a science.

My cousin Edward (Ned) McIlhenny Simmons, maternal great-grandson of Grandpère and current president of McIlhenny Company, continues the family tradition of personal involvement in every aspect of producing Tabasco sauce. Each fall he selects only the very best pepper seeds by walking the fields row by row, flipping a piece of twine onto each plant he selects. (This process was started long ago by his grandfather, who used Spanish moss instead of twine.) Ned looks for shape, color, size, and growth pattern, tagging about twelve hundred bushes in the process. Twenty pounds of seeds are taken from these plants, and some are actually stored in a New Iberia bank vault as insurance against possible future crop losses. Another fifty pounds are locked away in a vault at company headquarters.

Capsicum peppers growing on the same bush mature at different times, so a single bush may bear varying shades of green, yellow, and red peppers on a given day. Each pepper plant is picked several times during the harvest season by experienced pickers able to determine which peppers are at their peak of redness and ripeness. They are helped along by a "petit baton rouge," a stick painted the precise red of a perfectly ripe pepper.

Until the late 1960s we produced all of our peppers here on the island. Now more than 90 percent of our pepper crop is grown and harvested under our direct supervision in Honduras, Colombia, Venezuela, and the Dominican Republic. The pepper mash is shipped to Avery Island, where it is aged and then processed into sauce.

HOT PEPPER JELLY

||||

We generally make our pepper jelly with aged Tabasco pepper mash from the factory to give it color and flavor. Although perhaps not quite as fiery, this simple recipe using the pepper sauce makes a mellow, spicy jelly. Spread cream cheese on crackers, then top with a dollop of the jelly for a tempting morsel to serve with cocktails. Pectin is available in well-stocked supermarkets.

- 4 large red or green peppers, cored and seeded
- 1½ teaspoons Tabasco pepper sauce
- ¾ cup cider vinegar
- 3½ cups sugar
- 1 3-ounce pouch fruit pectin

Cut the peppers into large pieces, then coarsely chop in a food processor or blender. In a large nonaluminum saucepan over high heat, combine the peppers, Tabasco sauce, vinegar, and sugar. Bring to a boil and boil rapidly for 10 minutes, stirring occasionally. Remove from the heat and stir in the pectin. Return the pan to the heat and return to a boil. Boil the jelly for exactly 1 minute, then remove from the heat. Stirring frequently to prevent bits of pepper from rising to the surface, skim the foam off the top. Ladle the jelly into hot sterilized jars, seal, and place on a rack in a deep kettle. Pour boiling water over the jars to cover by 2 inches and bring to a boil over high heat. Continue to boil for 10 minutes, then remove to a rack to cool.

MAKES SIX 8-OUNCE JARS

ORANGE-KUMQUAT CHUTNEY

♦♦♦

Kumquats and oranges combine with a variety of aromatic ingredients to make this superb chutney. Keep it on hand to serve with meats, curry, game, or poultry. It also makes an attractive gift.

6 navel oranges
12 fresh kumquats (or 1 10-ounce jar preserved kumquats)
1 red pepper, seeded and chopped
1 green pepper, seeded and chopped
2 onions, chopped
1 cup raisins
2 cups cider vinegar
2 cups packed brown sugar
2 cinnamon sticks
½ teaspoon whole cloves
¼ cup diced crystallized ginger
1 tablespoon salt
2 teaspoons allspice
1½ teaspoons Tabasco pepper sauce

Cut the oranges into ¼-inch slices, remove any pits, and cut the slices into eighths. Cut the kumquats into ¼-inch slices. Put the oranges, kumquats, and remaining ingredients in a large heavy saucepan or kettle. Bring to a boil, stirring frequently. Reduce the heat and simmer, uncovered, for 1 hour, stirring occasionally. Ladle into clean jars, seal, and store in the refrigerator for up to 6 weeks.

MAKES 5 CUPS

SPICED PEACHES

The recipe may be simple, but these are a real treat when fresh peaches have gone out of season.

2 cups sugar
½ cup white vinegar
½ cup water
½ teaspoon Tabasco sauce
1 cinnamon stick
8 to 10 whole cloves
7 to 9 firm ripe peaches, peeled and halved, with stones removed

In a medium saucepan over high heat, combine the sugar, vinegar, water, Tabasco sauce, cinnamon, and cloves. Boil for 2 minutes, then add the peach halves. Boil for 10 minutes longer and remove from the heat. Let the peaches stand in the syrup for 30 minutes, then place in clean jars. Heat up the syrup again, pour over the peaches, and seal the jars. The peaches may be kept in the refrigerator for several weeks.

MAKES ABOUT 6 CUPS

TABASCO SAUCE IN DESSERTS?

Give desserts a new dash with Tabasco sauce. Add a teaspoon to your recipe for peanut butter, ginger, or sugar cookies. Sauté bananas in a combination of butter, brown sugar, honey, and a couple of drops of Tabasco sauce. Add a splash to chocolate or caramel sauce, or pour a Tabasco-laced curry sauce over ice-cold cut-up fruit for real taste excitement.

HOT SWEET PEARS

♦♦♦

These gingery pickled pears just get better on standing. Serve them with meats, game, duck, turkey, or chicken.

2	cups water
1⅓	cups white vinegar
2	cups apple juice
1	cup sugar
⅓	cup slivered fresh ginger
1½	teaspoons Tabasco pepper sauce
½	teaspoon salt
15	whole cloves
4	cinnamon sticks, 2-inch lengths
1	lime, thinly sliced
12	pears, cored, each cut into 8 wedges (Bosc, Bartlett, or Anjou)
1	cup raisins

In a large pot combine the water, vinegar, juice, sugar, ginger, Tabasco sauce, and salt. Tie the cloves, cinnamon sticks, and lime slices in a cheesecloth bag and add it to the pot. Cover the pot, bring to a simmer, and cook for 5 minutes. Add the pears and raisins. Cook over medium heat for 10 minutes, or until the pears are translucent but still firm. Discard the cheesecloth bag. Let the pears cool slightly, then cover and chill. The flavors will blend better if the pears are refrigerated for several days before using. The pears will keep in closed containers for several weeks in the refrigerator. Serve warm or at room temperature.

MAKES ABOUT 10 CUPS

Walter McIlhenny and Joseph Dubois "checking mash" in the early 1960s.

HOT PEPPERS COMBAT
THE COMMON COLD

People visiting the Tabasco sauce plant on Avery Island can expect to get their heads cleared when they take a whiff of the sauce being stirred. In fact, eating fiery foods can actually relieve congestion in the nose, sinuses, and lungs. Dr. Irwin Ziment, professor of medicine at the University of California in Los Angeles, recommends a glass of tomato juice laced with ten to twenty drops of Tabasco pepper sauce, taken several times daily as an excellent decongestant.

LEMON AND GARLIC GRILLING SAUCE

▮▮▮

TABASCO CLASSIC This is my favorite sauce for basting beef, chicken, or pork cooked on the grill or under the broiler. I often put the squeezed half lemon into the pot to simmer with the juice for extra flavor. In this and all recipes calling for Worcestershire sauce, I prefer Lea & Perrins, but you can make your own selection.

½ cup (1 stick) butter or margarine
½ lemon
1 tablespoon Worcestershire sauce
1½ teaspoons Tabasco pepper sauce
3 garlic cloves, minced
¼ teaspoon salt
Freshly ground black pepper to taste

In a medium nonaluminum saucepan over low heat, melt the butter. Squeeze the lemon juice into the pan and bring the mixture to a slow simmer. Add the Worcestershire sauce and Tabasco sauce. Stir in the garlic and continue to simmer for 10 minutes. Add the salt and pepper.

MAKES ¾ CUP

Hot Damn Green Sauce

||||

A variation on pesto, this recipe combines parsley, watercress, and basil in a sprightly sauce for cold cooked shrimp, salmon, carpaccio, or pasta.

    1   cup packed fresh parsley, rinsed and dried
    1   cup packed fresh watercress leaves, rinsed and dried
    1   cup packed fresh basil leaves, rinsed and dried
    ¼   cup pine nuts or almonds, toasted
    ¼   cup fresh lime juice
    ¼   cup olive oil
    2   small garlic cloves, minced
    1   teaspoon Tabasco pepper sauce

Combine all of the ingredients in a food processor or blender and process until smooth. Transfer the sauce to a covered container and chill for at least 24 hours to develop the flavor. Serve drizzled over chilled cooked shrimp, or warm the sauce and toss with hot pasta.

SERVES 4

AVERY ISLAND BARBECUE SAUCE

ıíı

TABASCO
CLASSIC This classic spicy barbecue sauce has a mellow, rich flavor that is marvelous with just about anything you'd care to grill. Serve additional sauce on the side.

    2 tablespoons butter or margarine
    1 cup chopped onion
    ½ cup chopped celery with leaves
    ¼ cup chopped green pepper
    1 tablespoon minced garlic
    2 14½-ounce cans whole tomatoes, drained and
         coarsely chopped
    1 6-ounce can tomato paste
    ⅓ cup red wine vinegar
    3 tablespoons molasses
    2 lemon slices
    2 teaspoons Tabasco pepper sauce
    2 teaspoons dry mustard
    1 bay leaf
    ½ teaspoon ground cloves
    ½ teaspoon ground allspice

In a large heavy nonaluminum saucepan over medium heat, melt the butter and sauté the onion, celery, pepper, and garlic for 5 minutes, or until the onion is tender but not browned. Add the remaining ingredients. Cover and simmer for 30 minutes, until the sauce thickens, stirring occasionally. Discard the lemon slices and bay leaf. Brush the sauce on chicken, ribs, frankfurters, or hamburgers during grilling, broiling, or baking.

MAKES 2 ¼ CUPS

RÉMOULADE SAUCE

Rémoulade sauce is another Louisiana specialty that varies with the cook. A piquant mustard-based sauce, it is excellent on cold shrimp or crab meat, and also goes nicely with hot, crisp fried fish or shellfish. Try it spooned over hard-boiled egg halves as an appetizer, or use it as a dip for cooked artichokes.

¼ cup spicy coarse-ground mustard
2 teaspoons paprika
1 teaspoon Tabasco pepper sauce
1 teaspoon salt
½ teaspoon freshly ground black pepper
¼ cup tarragon vinegar
1 cup olive oil
½ cup coarsely chopped green onions
½ cup finely chopped celery
¼ cup finely chopped fresh parsley

¼ teaspoon of Tabasco sauce gives a pleasing tang to Hollandaise, Béarnaise, or white sauce.

In a medium bowl, whisk together the mustard, paprika, Tabasco sauce, salt, and pepper. Beat in the vinegar and then, whisking constantly, add the oil in a slow, thin stream, continuing to beat until the sauce is thick and smooth. Stir in the green onions, celery, and parsley and mix well. Cover the bowl and let the sauce stand for at least 2 hours before serving to allow the flavors to blend.

MAKES 2 CUPS

CREAMY PEPPERY PASTA SAUCE

||||

We like this piquant tomato sauce, which is easy on the calories, but if you are in the mood to indulge, try cream in place of the ricotta and yogurt.

2 tablespoons olive oil
1 cup chopped onion
3 medium garlic cloves, minced
1 28-ounce can whole tomatoes
2 teaspoons Tabasco pepper sauce
1 tablespoon chopped fresh basil leaves or
    1 teaspoon dried
½ teaspoon dried rosemary
¼ teaspoon salt
⅓ cup ricotta cheese (see Note)
⅓ cup plain yogurt (see Note)

In a large saucepan, heat the oil and sauté the onion and garlic until soft, about 5 minutes. Chop the tomatoes, reserving the liquid. Add the tomatoes, ½ cup of the reserved liquid, and the Tabasco sauce, basil, rosemary, and salt to the saucepan and mix well. Simmer, uncovered, for 30 minutes, adding more of the tomato liquid if the sauce is too thick. In a food processor or blender, process the ricotta cheese and yogurt until smooth. Stir the mixture into the tomato sauce and heat without allowing it to come to a boil. The sauce may look slightly grainy, but appears smooth when it is added to hot pasta.

SERVES 4

NOTE: Low-fat ricotta and yogurt can be used.

Come Visit Us!

We welcome more than 100,000 visitors to Avery Island each year to see the Jungle Gardens and its famous Bird City, the new Tabasco visitors center, and the Tabasco Country Store. We greet each visitor personally and, after the tour, say good-bye with a *lagniappe* (small gift) of a miniature bottle of pepper sauce and a handful of recipes. The island is about 140 miles west of New Orleans, making it a pleasant day's trip through the bayou country.

MAIL ORDER SUPPLIES

Tabasco® brand and McIlhenny Farms®
brand products, assorted cookbooks, giftware, and
Cajun specialties:
TABASCO® Country Store
McIlhenny Company
Avery Island, LA 70513-5002
1 (800) 634-9599
Catalogue on request.

Crawfish, oysters, shrimp, crabs, frog legs,
alligator, sausages, and other Cajun products:

Randol's
2350 Kaliste Saloom Road
Lafayette, LA 70508
1 (800) YO CAJUN
FAX 1 (800) 962-2586

Bayou Land Seafood
1008 Vincent Berard Road
Breaux Bridge, LA 70517
(318) 667-7407
FAX (318) 667-6059

Noel Seafood
Route 5, Box 38
Abbeville, LA 70510
(318) 893-9494

Handy Soft Shell Crawfish
10557 Cherry Hill Avenue
Baton Rouge, LA 70816
(504) 292-4552

Sausages, other meats, and seasonings:

K-Paul's Louisiana Mail Order
824 Distributors Row
New Orleans, LA 70123
1 (800) 4KPAULS

Comeaux's Grocery
1000 Lamar Street
Lafayette, LA 70501
1 (800) 323-2492
1 (800) 737-2666

Venison:
Lucky Star Ranch
R.R.1., Box 273
Chaumont, NY 13622
(607) VENISON

Texas Wild Game Cooperative
P.O. Box 530
Ingram, TX 78025
1 (800) 962-4263

Game and game birds:
Balducci's
424 Avenue of the Americas
New York, NY 10011
(212) 673-2600

Muscadine jelly:
Callaway Gardens Country Store
Pine Mountain, GA 31822
(404) 663-5100

INDEX

Andouille and Chicken Gumbo, 56
Apricot-Curry Glazed Ribs, 91
Artichoke(s)
    dunk for, 24
    -Oyster Pan Roast, 64
    Potato and Leek Soup, 32
Asparagus, Lemon Sesame, 118

Barbecue Sauce, Avery Island, 138
Beans, 121. *See also* Red Beans;
    Trapper's Camp
Beef
    Chili, Walter McIlhenny's, 89
    Hamburger, Craig Claiborne's,
        88
    Steaks, Perfect Seared, 90
Bloody Mary, Classic, 51
Breakfast and Brunch, 36–52. *See
    also* Eggs; Cheese
    Chicken Hash, 44
    Corn Pudding, Fresh, 50
    Grillades for Brunch, 46
Buttermilk Beet Soup, 30

Cabbage Salad, Mellow, 102
Cajun Seafood Gumbo, 54
Capsicum (pepper), 61, 130
Carrot Parsnip Purée, 116
Carrots, Honey-Glazed, 112
Catfish Fingers, Fiery, 20
Cheese. *See also* Eggs
    Grits, 48
    Omelettes à la Suds, Rudy's, 36
    Scones, Parmesan, 106
    Torte, Herbed, 40
Chicken
    and Andouille Gumbo, 56
    Bites, Honey Mustard, 23
    Country Captain, 80
    Devil's, 83
    Hash, 44
    Olé Mole, 82
    Pot Pies, Individual, 84
    Wings, Hot 'N' Spicy, with Blue
        Cheese Dip, 26
Chili, Walter McIlhenny's, 89
Chutney, Orange-Kumquat, 132
Clams, Baked Cherrystone, 24
Clams, dunk for, 24
Cocktail sauce, 58
Condiment, 128–34. *See also* Sauce

Corn
    Maque Choux, 114
    Nips, 18
    Pudding, Fresh, 50
Courtbouillon, 73
Crawfish, 67; Etouffée, 66

Dirty Rice, 122
Duck, rare, 87

Eggplant New Iberia, 19
Eggs. *See also* Cheese
    Puffed-Up Omelette, 38
    Shirred, with Sherried
        Mushrooms, 37
Etouffée, Crawfish, 66

Fish
    Catfish Fingers, Fiery, 20
    Chowder, Vermillion Bay, 34
    Courtbouillon (Stew), 73
    Red Snapper Stew, 70
    Salmon Steaks with Cucumber
        Sauce, 75
    Steaks, Broiled, with Fresh
        Ginger Sauce, 72
    Trout, Hot Grilled, 74
Frog Legs Piquant, 68

Gazpacho, White Wine, 28
Green Beans, Zydeco, 119
Green Sauce, Hot Damn, 137
Grillades for Brunch, 46
Grilling Sauce, McIlhenny's, 136
Grits, Cheese, 48
Guacamole, 16
Gumbo, 57
    Cajun Seafood, Eula Mae's, 54
    Chicken and Andouille, 56

Hamburger, Craig Claiborne's,
    88

Jambalaya, 77; Eula Mae's, 76
Jelly, Hot Pepper, 131

Lamb
    Leg of, Mustard Crusted, 100
    Pepper-Stuffed, Garlic Chévre
        Sauce, 98
    Shanks in Red Wine, 96

Leek, Potato, Artichoke Soup, 32
Lemon Garlic Grilling Sauce, 136
Lobster, dunk for, 24

McIlhenny
    ads, early, 92
    family (and friends) photos, 42,
        45, 55, 63, 65, 135
    Judy, Crawfish Etouffée, 66
    Paul, Grilling Sauce, 136
    Walter, 29; Chili, 89
Muffins, Louisiana Yam, 108

Okra, 113; Creole Style, 113
Omelette. See Eggs
Onions, Piquant, 110
Orange-Kumquat Chutney, 132
Oyster-Artichoke Pan Roast, 64
Oyster Bisque, 33

Parsnip Carrot Purée, 116
Pasta Sauce, Creamy Peppery, 140
Pâté, Green Vegetable, 21
Peaches, Spiced, 133
Pears, Hot Sweet, 134
Pecans, Peppered, 14
Pepper. See Red Pepper
Polenta, Peppery, 124
Pork Ribs, Apricot-Curry, 91
Pork Roast, Gingered, 94
Potato(es)
    Artichoke and Leek Soup, 32
    Garlic-Roasted, 126
    Salad, Spanish, 115

Red Beans and Rice on Monday,
    123
Red Pepper Dip, Roasted, 15
Red Snapper Stew, 70
Rémoulade Sauce, 139
Rice, Dirty, 122
Roux, 59

Salad
    Cabbage, Mellow, 102
    Potato, Spanish, 115
    Sumatra, 103
Salmon Steaks with Cucumber
    Sauce, 75
Salsa, Chunky, 128
Sangrita, 52
Sauce, 136–40. See also Condiment;
    Tabasco sauce
    Avery Island Barbecue, 138
    Hot Damn Green, 137
    Lemon and Garlic Grilling, 136

Pasta, Creamy Peppery, 140
    Rémoulade, 139
Sausages, Herbed, in Wine, 25
Scallops, Double Pepper Sauce, 62
Scones, Parmesan Cheese, 106
Seafood. See also Name of Seafood
    Gumbo, Cajun, Eula Mae's, 54
Shallots, Pickled, 129
Shrimp
    Creole, 60
    Fred's Hottest, 58; Cocktail sauce
        for, 58
    Sauced, MTK's, 17
Soup, 28–34
    Buttermilk Beet, 30
    Cajun Seafood Gumbo, 54
    Chicken and Andouille Gumbo,
        56
    Fish Chowder, Vermillion Bay,
        34
    Oyster Bisque, 33
    Potato, Artichoke and Leek, 32
    White Wine Gazpacho, 28
    Zucchini-Cress, 31
Spareribs, Apricot-Curry, 91
Squash, Spirited, 104
Starters, 14–26
Steaks, Perfect Seared, 90
Stew. See also Gumbo
    Fish, Courtbouillon, 73
    Red Snapper, 70

Tabasco sauce, 9–11, 22, 105
    and beans, 121; at breakfast, 47;
    and cheese, 41; and the
    common cold, 135; in desserts,
    133; and eggs, 39; and grains,
    125; at lunchtime, 109; for
    meat, 97; notables who used,
    49; piquancy scale, 11; and
    seafood, 62; for soups, 31
Tomatoes, Herb Broiled, 117
Trapper's Camp Beans, 120
Trout, Hot Grilled, 74

Vegetable Pâté, Green, 21
Vegetable Salad, Sumatra, 103
Venison Chops Marchand de
    Muscadine, 86

Yam Muffins, Louisiana, 108

Zucchini-Cress Soup, 31